GOD IN ALL THINGS

GOD
IN ALL THINGS

A Manual of
Morning Worship in Schools

Lionel Fanthorpe

BISHOPSGATE PRESS

Fanthorpe, Lionel
  God in all things.
  1. Schools – Exercises and recreations
  2. Schools – Prayers
  I. Title
  377'.1   BV283.S3

ISBN 1-85219-001-9

All enquiries and requests relevant to this title should be sent to the publisher, Bishopsgate Press Ltd., 37 Union Street, London SE1 1SE

Printed by Whitstable Litho Ltd., Millstrood Road, Whitstable, Kent.

CONTENTS

11

15

DEDICATION

This book is lovingly dedicated to my Wife, Patricia, and our Daughters, Stephanie and Fiona, with tremendous gratitude for their unfailing help and support in preparing it, and in everything else. I know of no greater blessing than a Christian family united in a Christian home. I thank and praise God for them. **"As for me and my house, we will serve the Lord."**

Lionel Fanthorpe

FOREWORD

Few things worth doing are easy, but often they have to be done, and done to the best of our, perhaps, slender abilities. Many of us have striven for years to create an effective Act of Worship at the beginning of Sunday School, for example, or in the now so popular Family Services in Church, or day by day in the School Assembly in the Hall. Along with our own limitations, for all gifts are not automatically our birthright, we are faced with attention to catch and hold, a wide variety of ages and interests before us, and an atmosphere of relevance and sincerity to maintain, and **maintain** is the word to use for we have to live up to our standards, not once in a while but week by week over many years and for generations of children.

We can be no other than greatly indebted to those more gifted than ourselves who have been willing to share with us their research, their material, their method of working, and the skills that lie behind what they achieve. In this particular book we have the work of a convinced Christian who patently enjoys what he is seeking to do and who is only too glad to share his gifts with others. There is much here to help a great number of others and over many years.

"Worship," it is said, "is not only a duty which man owes to God; it is, when sincere and corporate, a refreshment and joy." It is sometimes hard to see School Assemblies in that light, but we would gladly make it so, and if Lionel Fanthorpe through his book helps us in any way to strengthen our worship, he will be more than grateful to Almighty God whose servants in this great aim we all of us are.

Canon S.H. Mogford, M.A.

INTRODUCTION

This is a collection of fifty-two short services – one for every week of the year – or for use whenever they are required.

The basic idea behind the collection is to relate each service to an experience, or an idea, which will be familiar to school students.

For example, one service refers to English, another to Mathematics, another to Pottery; one is concerned with the Library, while another relates to shopping, buying and selling. The overall idea is to show that true religion embraces every part of our lives: **all things** can teach us about God.

Each service follows the same order because there is much to be said for establishing a regular pattern of worship for the School Assembly. There is a theme title, followed by a relevant Scripture reading with its Key Verse, and an appropriate hymn. Then follows a short passage which can either be read just as it stands, or used as the basis of a shorter, or longer, talk at the speaker's discretion – depending upon the time available and the circumstances of the individual school. The material can also be used for regular R. E. Lessons, for Sunday School work, for Young People's Services and for Family Worship.

It is presented to Christian teachers, preachers, speakers, youth leaders and ministers in the hope that some small part of it may be of service to them, to those whom they lead in worship, and, above all, to the Lord Jesus Christ whom we all serve.

Lionel Fanthorpe
Cardiff, 1987

CHAPTER 1

Time and Events
God in History

Scripture Reading: Ecclesiastes 3:1-8

Key verse: Ecclesiastes 3 verse 1: To every thing there is a season, and a time to every purpose under heaven.

Hymn: O God, our help in ages past, (Isaac Watts, 1674–1748).

There are two rival theories about the nature of history. One suggests that there are great tides of events : economic changes, political and technological changes on which men and women are swept along helplessly like autumn leaves on a flooded river. The other theory suggests that great men and women make momentous decisions which can turn the social tides and steer the course of history.

As Christians, we know that however difficult it is to understand the problems, disasters and tragedies of history, God is still there at the back of all things. Jesus Himself said that even the death of a sparrow does not take place without God's knowledge and concern.

We look at time and the stream of events which we call history from the inside. When you are a passenger travelling in a bus your view of the road is very different from the view you would get from a plane or a mountain peak. Looking down from a great height above the road you can see where the bus has been and where it's going. Looking at time from the point of view of eternity is like having an aerial view of the road. Looking at time from the point of view of time is like being a passenger in the bus.

Now suppose that the roads over which the bus is travelling branch and fork and cross one another repeatedly. At each junction the driver has a choice of ways. But the driver is influenced in his choice by many factors. He has a route and time-table to follow. He may be driving fast because he is anxious to get home for supper. He may be new to this route and looking carefully at all the signposts and landmarks along the way. He may be old, or tired, or not feeling very well, and driving slowly and cautiously. Perhaps there is an inspector, or bus company manager, on board, giving the driver instructions. Perhaps the passengers are arguing with the driver about which way to go, or where and when to stop. The driver is not completely free to make his own decisions. He is influenced and affected by other people. Some drivers will be more easily influenced than others. Some, with strong personalities and clear ideas of their own, will hardly be influenced at all. Drivers who make wrong decisions will get lost, or will cause disasters, and may well involve many other people in their disasters. History is often a record of wrong decisions and the tragedies that followed.

Whether we see ourselves as drivers or passengers on the roads of history, we each have a part to play. Even though our influence may be very small, each one of us has **some** influence over events. Let us be determined on three things: one, to seek God's will for our lives; two, to try our best to go the way that God wants us to go; and, three, to do our best to influence others in the right direction by speaking and acting fearlessly for what we believe to be right.

Prayer:

O Lord of time and eternity, whose almighty power controls the lives and destinies of all men and nations, help us to play our part faithfully, be it large or small. Help us to understand Your will, to know what is right, and to do it with courage and gladness, through Jesus Christ our Lord, Amen.

CHAPTER 2

Lands and Seas
God in Geography

Scripture Reading: Deuteronomy 28:1-10

Key verse: Deuteronomy 28 verse 10: And all people of the earth shall see that thou art called by the name of the Lord.

Hymn: Jesus shall reign where'er the sun, (Isaac Watts, 1674–1748).

There was a time when the majority of people probably spent most of their lives in their home town or village. Travel was slow, difficult, dangerous and very expensive. Nowadays we say that the speed and convenience of modern transport have made the world shrink. Places that once seemed remote are only a few hours' flying time away. We plumb the depths of oceans and climb the highest mountains. We navigate strange seas and build roads across jungles and deserts. The inaccessible places of the world are becoming known. Nations and tribes which once knew little or nothing of one another's existence are now next door neighbours because of radio, television, satellites and supersonic aircraft. Africans, Asians, Europeans, Eskimos, Russians and Americans all know far more about one another's homelands than ever before.

Geography teaches us about the rocks, the rivers, the soil and the mountains, the lakes, seas and oceans of our world. We learn about climatic extremes: equatorial jungles and polar ice caps, rainforests and deserts, fertile farmlands and poisonous swamps.

Geography also teaches us about people and populations and what they **do** with the land they live on. We learn about mining and minerals, fishing and forestry, agriculture and industry, imports and exports, docks and railways, shipbuilding, oil refineries and hydro-electric power.

There is an old North American Indian proverb: "Never judge a man until you have walked for a day in his moccasins." Learning as much as we can about other people and their ways of living helps us to see life from their point of view and to understand them better. Each time we study other lands in our geography lessons we are taking the first few steps in someone else's moccasins.

It is clearly part of the will of God, the loving heavenly Father of all races and all nations, that his children all over the world should live as one great family of brothers and sisters. We should be willing to accept the help and advice of our brothers and sisters across the sea, and to offer our help and advice whenever it is requested. In Christ there is neither east nor west, black nor white, Jew nor Gentile, Greek nor barbarian. He does not see first, second or third worlds, but one world, and that is His world.

Prayer:

Our loving Lord, Creator of all men, all races and all nations, help us today and every day to learn more and to understand more about our brothers and sisters in other lands. Help us, Lord, in this our land, and in other lands far away, to know You as Father of us all, and so to love and help one another for the sake of Him who died to save us all, Jesus Christ our Lord, Amen.

CHAPTER 3

Glass, Timber and Stone
God in our Buildings

Scripture Reading: Matthew 7:21-29

Key verse: Matthew 7 verse 24: Whosoever heareth these sayings of mine, and doeth them, I will liken him unto a wise man, which built his house upon a rock.

Hymn: O God, the Rock of Ages, (Edward Henry Bickersteth, 1825–1906). (Recommended Tune: "Aurelia" by S. S. Wesley, 1810–76).

The meaning of our Lord's teaching about building on rock or building on sand is very clear. Unless the foundations of our lives are resting securely on God, the Rock of Ages, our lives will be worth very little, and we shall not be able to withstand the many dangers and difficulties of life.

But once we have chosen that Divine Rock, the only secure foundation, what shall we build, and what materials shall we use?

There's a famous old story, which you'll all have known well since infant school, about three pigs who built their houses of straw, wood and brick respectively. When the wolf arrived he very quickly destroyed the straw house and the pig who'd built it ran to his brother in the wooden house for shelter. The wolf dealt with the wooden house as well, and the two terrified pigs then ran to the third brother, who'd built the sturdy and solid house of bricks. This defied all the wolf's efforts, and, depending upon which version of the story you were told as an infant, he either died of exhaustion, or burst, while trying to blow the brick house down, or he tried to get down the chimney and died in a large cauldron of boiling water which the pigs had prepared for him. The point of that story was that it's well worth going to the extra effort and trouble of building a house of brick or stone. Wood and straw may be cheap, quick, and easy to use, but they offer only poor protection when danger threatens.

Once we've made the major decision, and founded our lives on God's Eternal Rock, we must still think carefully about the kind of structures we want our lives to be. The Rock of Ages will never move. It will never fail us. But if we build only a thin, flimsy structure upon it, we shall be failing ourselves.

When we look around at earthly buildings we see brick, stone, concrete, steel, glass, timber and plastic. Each material has its strengths and its weaknesses. Steel is very strong and durable, but in a swimming pool roof laminated timber beams are often used instead of steel because wood can withstand the chlorine in the atmosphere better than the steel can. Some materials – such as glass or polycarbonate – are excellent for admitting light, but they tend to let out heat in cold weather and to let in too much sunlight in summer.

Each material is best suited to a particular purpose. The right material in the wrong place causes problems. Roofing tiles, or slates, must be light as well as strong and waterproof. When we select the material from which to build our lives on the Eternal Rock of God's goodness, we need to choose appropriate ones. If God is calling someone to be a Missionary, he or she needs to build into his or her life the skills to write and speak the languages of those with whom he or she hopes to work overseas.

As Christians we all need to build the bricks of kindness and courtesy into the fabric of our lives' buildings. We need the steel of courage. We need the warmth and friendliness of wood. We need the incorruptibility of plastic. We need the clearness of glass.

Prayer:

O Lord, the Eternal Rock upon Whom we build our lives, grant us the wisdom to build wisely and well. Teach us what to do in order to make the best of our lives and the most of our opportunities, so that we shall be acceptable to You and to our fellow Christians. We ask it in and through the Name of the One who is acceptable in Your sight, Jesus Christ the Righteous, Amen.

CHAPTER 4

The Good and the Beautiful
God in Art

Scripture Reading: Chronicles 3:3-14

Key verse: Chronicles 3:6: And he garnished the house with precious stones for beauty.

Hymn: O thou not made with hands (F. T. Palgrave 1824–1897).

Let us think about art and decoration, and all the different ways in which we can express our ideas artistically. We can use pencil, crayon, charcoal, pastels, pen and ink, water-based paints, oil paints, acrylic, air-brushes and many other things to create shape and form. We can take needles and canvas and embroider our designs. We can tie cloth, dip it in dye and create designs in that way. We can carve lino and make prints. We can make woodcuts and steel-engravings. We can etch; we can carve; we can kiln pottery. We can take photographs. Gardeners can lay out flower-beds and even whole landscapes. Architects can design beautiful buildings, like King Solomon's Temple which we read about this morning, or our own lovely cathedrals and abbeys, churches and chapels. The imaginative artist chooses his or her material and asks: "How can I make this into something beautiful and worthwhile?"

The most important material we have to work with is our own life. We are all artists: whether we can draw or paint, mould or carve in the art and craft lessons, we all have the responsibility of making something of ourselves. Now, just as clay and wood are very different, just as steel and paper are different, so our media, the raw materials of our lives, are different. We were born at different times and in different places. Some of us are older than others. Some of us have experienced more of life than others. Some of us are bold and adventurous. Some of us may be timid and shy. We are tall or short, heavy or light, energetic or quiet. Each one of us is a distinct individual, mentally and physically. You and I are the material which God our Father has given us, and it is our responsibility to Him, and to ourselves, to make the most of that gift.

An artist can choose not to paint. He can leave the paint on the palette until it dries up and becomes useless. An artist can make mistakes. He can create designs which are crude, ugly and evil. That is his choice. We can do the same with our lives. We can decide to do

26

nothing with them. We can waste them, like unused paint on the artist's palette. We can deliberately go in the wrong direction. We can make wrong decisions, weak decisions, bad decisions. When an artist has made a wrong decision he can take a new sheet of paper or canvas and begin again. When an artist is tired of wasting his time, he can clean his palette, squeeze new paint from the tubes and start to do some worthwhile work. Jesus Christ can do this for us.

Sometimes in your art or craft lesson you can't get the design right. You have a good idea, but you have difficulty in expressing it. Your art teacher helps and advises you, shows you how to make the best of your idea, how to reach your objective. Sometimes the teacher will give you a new sheet of paper, a new piece of clay, a new piece of wood or metal to work on. This is what Jesus does with our lives. Deep within us we have an urge to do better, to be the kind of men and women He wants us to be: to be honest, truthful, kind, courageous, gentle and good. But we all experience difficulties. We give in to one temptation or another. We are not always honest. We are not always completely truthful. We are arrogant, selfish and unkind. We are afraid when we should be brave. We are cruel when we should be gentle. That is when we need Jesus most. Just as we ask the art teacher to help us to get our picture right, we need Jesus to help us to get our lives right. The Divine Artist can make our pictures represent His Truth, if we ask Him. He gives us another sheet of paper: the gift of a new day, the fresh opportunity to give our lives to Him, and become new people in Him.

Prayer:

O God, our loving Father, who sent our Lord Jesus Christ into this world to save sinners, and to restore them to You, help us to think of our lives as work we are doing for You, and help us to commit that work to You. Be with us, Lord, in all that we do, all that we say, and all that we think. Guard us and guide us in all things, and make us acceptable, not because of our merits, but because of His Merits, through our same Lord, Jesus Christ, Amen.

CHAPTER 5

Persistence
God on the Sea-shore

Scripture Reading: Luke 11:5-13
Key verse: Luke 11:9: Ask and it shall be given you.
Hymn: He who would valiant be (John Bunyan, 1628–1688. Adapted by P. Dearmer, 1867–1936).

If you go to the beach at Winterton, a seaside village in North Norfolk, and walk towards the west, you will see the solid new concrete sea-defences designed to protect the dunes and the land behind them. There are notices above the concrete ramparts asking visitors not to walk on the newly planted marram grass. The scientific, botanical name for marram is **Ammophila arenaria** or **Ammophila brevilgulata,** and its most important characteristic is that it puts out many tough rhizomes – runners which are able to produce both shoots and new roots. As the marram spreads across the sand its powerful rhizomes bind the dunes firmly together, strengthening the sea defences. In many parts of the world marram is an essential part of coastal defences – especially in areas like Norfolk, or Holland, where the land is flat and close to sea level.

As you walk along the beach and look at the spreading marram, you will be surprised by how tough and persistent it is. The sand is bleak, salty and inhospitable, but the marram spreads through it. The tides break up against the dunes. Shells and stones are carried over the new rhizomes. Holidaymakers walk on them. Children build sandcastles over them. Dogs chase sticks across them, and scrape the sand away. Fishermen drag their boats and tackle past. Land Rovers drive over the new plants – but the marram holds on.

Sir Thomas Buxton, who lived from 1786 until 1845, was a great fighter against the slave trade, like the more famous William Wilberforce. Sir Thomas was married to Hannah Gurney, sister of the famous Elizabeth Fry, the great prison reformer. One of the things Sir Thomas said reminds us of the strength and persistence of the marram grass in our coastal defences:-

"The longer I live, the more I am certain that the great difference between men – between the feeble and the powerful, the great and the insignificant – is energy, **invincible determination,** a purpose once fixed, and then death or victory!"

Ray Kroc, who purchased the McDonald name from two brothers who ran a small restaurant in San Bernardino, California, also knew the importance of persistence. Kroc was originally a restaurant equipment salesman, who became a multi-millionaire after starting the world-famous McDonald franchising business. Ray Kroc said that nothing in this world was as great a weapon as persistence. He said that determination and persistence could overcome all obstacles. A Texan oil man once said that the simple secret of his success was **to go on drilling** when the others had given up. There is the famous lesson of King Bruce of Scotland and the spider. The spider would not give up trying to spin its web, even though it fell time and again from the damp and difficult surface of the cave wall. At last the spider succeeded. Bruce learnt a vital lesson from watching it, and he, too, went on to try again, and to succeed. In the old pantomime story of Dick Whittington, young Whittington, very discouraged, is leaving London, depressed and disappointed, when he hears the bells. They seem to be telling him to turn back to the city and to try once more. As we all know, he finally became Lord Mayor. Marram grass or men: the message is the same – **persist. Never give up.** The only barriers we cannot pass are the ones we set up for ourselves.

Jesus Himself has told us to knock, and life's doors will be opened for us. He has told us to ask God, our Father, and we shall receive. He has told us to seek and we shall find. These are not mere words. These are not proverbs, or pieces of good advice. These are the solemn promises of our Lord Jesus Christ Himself, as recorded in the Scriptures. They are addressed to us today just as directly as they were addressed to his disciples and followers nearly 2,000 years ago. These words live. These promises are true – and they are relevant for us. If we knock on the door of Life, Christ will open it for us. If we seek God's salvation we shall find it. If we ask for God's gift of life, we shall receive it. But we must be like the marram grass. We must be persistent, strong and resolute. God our Father never fails. Jesus never fails. It is only when we are tempted to give up that we are in danger of failing ourselves.

Prayer:

O loving and eternal Lord, help us to be steadfast and persistent for all that is right, and good, and true. Father, You know us better than we know ourselves. You know our weaknesses, our lack of stamina and our failure to persist. Grant to each one of us that strength of mind, body and will, that enables us to do what You would have us do, and be what You would have us be, this day and every day, for Jesus' sake, Amen.

CHAPTER 6

Recreation
God in Rest and Enjoyment

Scripture Reading: Isaiah 56:6-8 and Luke 13:10-17
*Key verse: Luke 13:17: And all the people rejoiced for all the glorious
things that were done by him.*
Hymn: Come let us with our Lord arise, (Charles Wesley, 1707–1788).

A very few wise men have the capacity to understand. Most of the
rest of us are experts at misunderstanding. Worst of all, many of us
seem to misunderstand with the best of intentions and with great
enthusiasm. The Sabbath Day – God's Day of rest and refreshment
– has been misunderstood and misinterpreted by many who have
sought genuinely to serve Him throughout the ages. Only our Lord
Jesus Christ understood it perfectly, as He understood all things.
Our Father and Maker knows far more about human beings than we
know about ourselves. He knows more about our bodies than the
most skilful professor of medicine. He knows more about our minds
than the most highly qualified psychologist. God our Maker knows
that we need rest and relaxation at regular intervals. He knows that
all of us – even the toughest and the most energetic – cannot go on
without a rest. When we have the sense to listen to and understand
His Word then we take that rest and relaxation on the Lord's Day.
When we respect a doctor, we take his advice about our health. If he
says, "Get more exercise," then we do it. If he says, "Take less salt
and sugar," then we do that, too. It is a sign of respect for our doctor,
an indication of our confidence in him and his professional
knowledge, when we follow his advice. Our loving Father deserves
far more respect than we give to the very best doctor. Our Father's
instructions are that we should keep and honour His Holy Day once
a week, but how often is that divine instruction disobeyed? How
often is it misunderstood?

The original Sabbath in Israel was a very good and humane day of
rest: as all God's commandments can be seen to be good and
humane when we take the time to study them closely. The Sabbath
ensured that servants and slaves in ancient Israel were not worked
selfishly and without rest by their masters. How often do we all –
staff and students alike – look forward to Friday, or to the end of
term? Imagine being a slave, or the servant of a hard, selfish master,
who gave you no rest at all. Imagine a life of toil in which there were
no week-ends, no holidays, no rest days. Unfortunately, as years
passed, the Scribes and Pharisees and so-called 'experts' in the

Jewish Law, changed the emphasis of the Sabbath Law. They became very concerned by what did, or did not, count as 'work' for legal purposes. One day when Jesus and the Disciples were walking through a corn field, the Disciples were plucking off ears of corn and rubbing the grains out in their hands to eat. The Scribes and Pharisees criticised them for 'working', that was, technically, threshing corn, on the Sabbath! The Scribes and Pharisees also criticised Jesus Himself for healing on the Sabbath, and their stubbornness and spiritual blindness made Him very angry indeed. Jesus, with unique spiritual wisdom and keen insight into His Father's will and purpose, knew that the Sabbath was made for the benefit of mankind, and not the other way round. Over and over again he pointed out to the Scribes and Pharisees that God was served best by kindness and love towards others. The Sabbath had been given that men might have the rest they needed. When Jesus healed people, He gave them rest from the diseases that were ruining their lives. His healing touch was a Sabbath blessing indeed. We need to keep our Lord's special teaching about the Sabbath clearly in our minds whenever we think of how to spend the Lord's Day. Our rest and relaxation need to be dedicated to God just as much as our work.

God, our loving Father, wants us to be happier than we can ever begin to imagine. We can only find that happiness – in work or recreation – when we obey His Laws. It is not in keeping with the spirit of the Lord's Day to do any unnecessary work, anything that could perfectly well be left for another time. It is not in keeping with the spirit of the Lord's Day to do anything that obliges others to work unnecessarily on that Day. It is in keeping with God's Law to do anything that helps, heals, or brings joy to others in the Lord's Name on His Day. Repairing your car on a Sunday in order to have it roadworthy to take an elderly neighbour to see her family for Sunday tea, or to take her to her church to enjoy the fellowship of her friends while she worships, is a joyful duty. Repairing your car on a Sunday, when you could have done it on Saturday but went fishing instead, is not justified.

Prayer:

Lord of all our time, Lord of all we do, Lord of all our work and Lord of all our leisure, help us so to love and serve You, that we may be partakers of that mind which was in Christ Jesus our Lord. Help us to understand and respect Your Day, as He did, that by our actions on Your Day we may bring ourselves and others closer to You, through Jesus Christ our Saviour, Amen.

CHAPTER 7

Food and Drink
God in Bread and Wine

Scripture Reading: Luke 22:7-20

Key verse: Luke 22 verse 19: And He took bread, and gave thanks, and brake it and gave unto them.

Hymn: Bread of the world in mercy broken, (Bishop R. Heber, 1783–1826).

When we pause and consider the things we so often take for granted, we find that these simple, everyday things are often the most wonderful. Most of us will have eaten breakfast of some kind today. Many of those breakfasts will have contained bread. We have probably eaten a piece of bread almost every day of our lives. It is such a simple, natural part of our diet that we hardly give it a second thought.

But when we study bread-making as part of our Home Economics or Domestic Science Course, when we study the bread-making process as part of a Catering Course, as they do in some schools and colleges, when we look at yeast and fermentation as part of our work in biology and general science, we begin to see that this apparently simple, 'taken-for-granted' daily food is far from ordinary.

The processes by which modern varieties of high protein milling wheat are selected, grown, marketed, manufactured and distributed are very complex. The wrapped, sliced loaf on the shelf in the shop has come a long, long way since the grains of seed wheat were planted.

Yet God's providence and God's Law is there from the beginning to the end: God is the same loving Father of the farmer who plants the corn, of the miller, of the baker, of the shopkeeper, and of the man or woman who buys the finished loaf. If each man, or woman, in that team does his, or her, part honestly, caringly and responsibly, thinking as much of God's other children as of themselves – in accordance with Christ's teachings – then the bread will be pure and wholesome, and priced fairly for all to buy.

That same principle applies to everything we buy to eat and drink. Those of you who work part-time in shops and supermarkets might like to think about your own special part in that food distributing team, and consider how it fits in with all the rest. What are your special responsibilities to others?

Jesus used simple, everyday things like bread and wine to reveal the most profound spiritual truths. God is with us in the planting of the corn, in the growing of the wheat and in the Breaking and Sharing of the Bread. God gives us so much more than the daily food we need to sustain our physical bodies. In the Lord Jesus Christ, He gives us His Son, and, as Jesus explained to the Disciples when He shared the bread and wine, the gift of the Son is the gift of eternal life.

Prayer

Loving heavenly Father, we thank You for the simplicity and ordinariness of the everyday world, and for the Divine Mysteries which lie unseen behind it. Open our spiritual eyes so that we may give true thanks for the Bread of Life each time that we eat our daily bread here on earth, through Jesus Christ our Lord, who gives us that same Bread of Everlasting Life, Amen.

CHAPTER 8

Law, Order and the Constitution
God in Justice and Mercy

Scripture Reading: Exodus 20:1-17

Key verse: Exodus 20 verse 6 : ...shewing mercy unto thousands of them that love me and keep my commandments.

Hymn: Eternal Ruler of the ceaseless round (J. W. Chadwick, 1840–1904).

When a yacht is sailing on a course contrary to the wind, the yacht has to tack doggedly from side to side in order to make any headway at all. You can often see this happening on inland rivers and waterways like the Norfolk Broads, when the yachtsmen have to tack from one bank to another. It is only by tacking like that from one bank to the other that the sailors can make progress up or down the river. The banks are limits, or guide-lines. The true course along the river itself lies between them. It is often difficult for a helmsman to know exactly when to turn his vessel and to sail on the other tack. The opposite banks seem different, yet both are undoubtedly part of the same river. The Thames would not be the Thames if it had only a north bank or only a south bank.

The Justice of God and the Mercy of God are equally part of the Nature of God as it is revealed to us in Scripture. Jesus forgave penitent sinners – even the dying thief who was crucified beside Him – but he used a whip to drive the money-changers from the Temple, and hurled their tables over. He said that only those who were without sin themselves were entitled to throw the first stone at the woman who had sinned, but he also proclaimed God's sternest judgement against those scribes and Pharisees who were formalists and hypocrites, blind guides who led others into danger. Jesus did not preach peace at any price, but righteousness at any cost – even to death on the cross. He once told the Disciples that the man who didn't have a sword should sell his cloak to buy one, and He also told a parable about a strong man, armed, keeping his house safe.

Unfortunately, there are many people today who have misunderstood this vital balance between justice and mercy. Sadly, they seem to think that because Christians are told by their Lord to be merciful that wrong-doing can be condoned, excused or ignored.

Yet true love must be prepared to punish, to correct, and to guide, when necessary, as well as to forgive. Jesus did not condone, ignore, or excuse the money-changers who were defiling God's House – He drove them out. Jesus did not ignore or excuse the sinful woman – He showed great mercy but He told her clearly: "Sin no more." Jesus did not excuse the formalism and hypocrisy of the Scribes and Pharisees. He told them what they were, and He warned them severely of God's coming judgement.

Without **both** its banks, a river would not be a river. Without Divine Justice **as well as** Divine Mercy – the Mercy that died on the cross to save us – God would not be God. It is at the Cross that Justice and Mercy stand together to reveal the awe-inspiring mystery of the Saving Love of God.

Prayer:

Great Heavenly Father, grant us so to understand both Justice and Mercy, that we may always strive to keep Your Divine Law. Help us to be strong without being proud, to be merciful without being weak, and to be just without being harsh, for the sake of Him in whom Perfect Justice and Perfect Mercy dwell for ever more, Christ Jesus our Lord, Amen.

CHAPTER 9

Melody and Harmony
God in Music

Scripture Reading: Psalm 33:1-9

Key verse: Psalm 33 verse 1: Rejoice in the Lord, O ye righteous.

Hymn: Come let us join our cheerful songs (Isaac Watts, 1674–1748).

Over and over again Scripture tells us to rejoice in the Lord. Worship is a good and happy thing. It is a cause for gladness and celebration. It is a time for singing, for dancing, and for playing musical instruments. We worship God because He created us, He sustains us, and He has opened the Door of Eternal and Abundant Life for us in the Person and Work of His Son, Jesus Christ. This is good news indeed! It is the greatest, the most exciting and the most important Good News that anyone will ever hear. God is love! Jesus lives! We can live, too, **forever**, because of Him! That is something to sing about in our hymns. That is something to rejoice over in our music. That is something to give eternal thanks for in our prayers and praises.

Music is a good gift and a great talent, yet it is a gift that can be badly misused, and a talent that can easily be wasted. It can be turned in wrong directions, or wasted on trivia. In order to be good, music does not have to be 'classical', or 'operatic', or 'pop', or 'rock' or 'jazz' or 'country and western' or to fit into any other category. Musical names, styles and fashions change all the time. In order to qualify as **good**, music must **serve** the good. We know that God is the Absolute Good, so good music is music which is dedicated to God and glorifies Him.

We glorify God in music when we employ whatever musical talents He has given us to the full and to the utmost. God wants the **best** we can do and the **most** we can do – it is as simple and as difficult as that. The best music is directly concerned with praising and worshipping God: Handel's "Messiah", for example, or some of the great hymns we sing. Those stirring marches which are characteristics of the Salvation Army, Country and Western Gospel Songs from Nashville, Tennessee, or Christian Blues from the Southern States of the U.S.A. are all saying something uniquely important about God in their own special ways.

36

"Amazing Grace" played by a solitary piper at sunset in a remote Highland Glen, Bach's fugues played to a crowded congregation and the hymns we sing at school or in church are all equally acceptable to God our Father, provided that all of us do the best we can and the most we can with the musical ability He has given us.

Prayer:

Our loving heavenly Father, we thank You for the gift of music, for harmony and melody, for voices and musical instruments. We thank You for the joys of playing, singing and listening. Help us always to offer You the best we can do and the most we can do, in our music and in every part of our lives, for Jesus' sake, Amen.

CHAPTER 10

Striving and Endeavour
God in Sport and Recreation

Scripture Reading: Philippians 3:9-17

Key verse: Philippians 3 verse 14: I press towards the mark for the prize of the high calling of God in Christ Jesus.

Hymn: Fight the good fight with all thy might (J. S. B. Monsell, 1811–1875).

Let us think of some of the different ways in which we can compete on the sports field, against the clock, against the scales, against the tape-measure, against other players or against our own previous best. We read in Scripture of how strong men rejoice to run a race, and it is enjoyable to take part in sports, gymnastics and athletics. Sportsmen throw the hammer, javelin and the discus. They put the shot. They leap over heights and over distances. They bound over hurdles. They sprint for short distances and pound away doggedly at marathons. They race on skates, on skis, and in sledges. They swim; they dive; they climb; they lift weights; they tug ropes; they wrestle and box. They sail boats and ride horses. They row; they glide; they parachute; they guide canoes through white water. They strive and they dare in a hundred different ways. Why do they do it?

For some it is ambition. They want to be first. They want to be best. They want to beat everyone else. They want to be record holders. For others it is the sheer love of the sport itself. They enjoy the activity, or the thrill, for its own sake.

For some, sport is an escape from unhappy or unsuccessful life situations. The computer programmer, the shop keeper, the banker, the lorry driver and the factory machinist may be unfulfilled at work, but much happier at their Judo club. Many sportsmen and women have gone on to become champions after taking up their sport in the first place to get fit and strong again after some accident or illness.

Whatever our sport, and whatever our original reason for taking it up, there are important spiritual lessons to be learnt from it. God gave us our bodies, our strength, and our energy, be they small or great, to use in His service. We can praise God in the simple act of enjoying our physical fitness, developing it to the full, and thanking Him for it. We can always be on the look-out for opportunities to use our health, strength and energy to help others, especially those who are less fortunate.

In sport, even the best athletes – the Olympic Champions and the World Record Holders – are constantly seeking to improve their own best performances.

In the spiritual life, the truly great Christians – those who walk closest to Christ, do most for others, and think least of their own needs – are always striving to do better still for His sake.

In sport, the greatest satisfaction comes from competing honestly, keeping the rules, playing fairly. Winning by cheating is far worse than losing.

In the spiritual life the deepest joys come from keeping God's laws and living as Christ would have us live.

Prayer:

O Lord, our Father, You have given us all good sports and leisure activities; help us to enjoy them in the right way. As we strive in games and athletics, help us also to strive in our work and in the world outside – fairly, honestly, generously, and in accordance with Your Laws. May we always put You first, others second and ourselves last, for the sake of Him who strove with and overcame evil that we might live, Jesus Christ our Lord, Amen.

CHAPTER 11

Small Things and Great
God in the Details

Scripture Reading: Matthew 10:26-34

Key verse: Matthew 10 verse 30: But the very hairs of your head are all numbered.

Hymn: For the beauty of the earth, (F. S. Pierpoint, 1835–1917).

There are many stories told of David Lloyd George, the famous Welsh Prime Minister, and one of them concerns a remark he is said to have made to explain his political success.

"While I am tying my shoe-laces, nothing else in the world matters until they are properly tied. If I did not have that ability, Lloyd George would still be an unknown Welsh farmer." When the leader of a Government can take so much care over a detail like tying his shoe-laces, we can learn much from him about the importance of details.

George Herbert (1593–1633) included a short version of the fable about the loss of one horse-shoe nail which led to disaster in his collection of proverbs entitled "Jacula Prudentum", published in 1651.

> For want of a nail, the shoe was lost.
> For want of a shoe, the horse was lost.
> For want of a horse, the rider was lost.
> For want of the rider, the message was lost.
> For want of the message, the battle was lost.
> For want of the battle, the kingdom was lost –
> And all for the want of a horse-shoe nail.

When we are writing an English essay, or composition, we may have a good, clear style and a logically connected flow of interesting ideas, but if we neglect the details of spelling and punctuation we are not going to get a very high mark for that piece of work. When we are calculating, we may deal quickly and accurately with large numbers and complex processes, but if we forget to change a sign from a minus to a plus, or write x when we mean y, we shall not reach the correct answer. Here again, details are very important.

When we are measuring a piece of metal, counting stitches,

matching colours or weighing chemicals, attention to accuracy and fine detail is essential for success.

A thoughtful look around the Universe – out to the most distant galaxies and in to the smallest sub-atomic particles – will soon show us our Father's concern for details.

Everywhere we look we find the greatest intricacy and detail in God's creation. Snowflakes have patterns. The smallest leaves are delicately veined.

As God our Father is so concerned with detail, we should learn to look carefully at detail as well. There are many small but very important parts of the Christian life, things like courtesy, politeness and cheerfulness – being friendly and helpful in the details of everyday life – which make the world an altogether more Christian place for those we share it with day by day.

Prayer:

Our loving Heavenly Father, we know from Your Word that You are always aware of the smallest details of our lives, and that You are lovingly concerned with the lesser events as well as the greater ones. Help us observe the detail in Your Creation, and so to live that every part of our lives – every smallest thought and action – is acceptable in Your sight, through Jesus Christ our Lord, Amen.

CHAPTER 12

Travel and Change
God in our Journeyings

Scripture Reading: Exodus 13:17-22

Key verse: Exodus 13 verse 21: And the Lord went before them.

Hymn: Guide me, O thou great Redeemer (W. Williams, 1717–1791).

When we analyse our lives moment by moment, we are often surprised by the amount of time we spend travelling. We may walk to school in the morning, home again at lunch-time, back to school in the afternoon, and home again at tea-time. If we take ten minutes for each journey, that's forty minutes each day spent in travelling. That's about the length of a lesson. If we could spend five extra lessons a week on a subject we should expect to do well at it. If we could spend forty minutes a day on homework or revision, it would certainly improve our examination results. Time spent in travelling isn't wasted. We have to get from one place to another, but all time has an opportunity cost. While we are doing one thing, we cannot be doing another **at the same time.** We cannot choose to do English homework **and** Maths homework simultaneously. We cannot choose to watch television and play rugby **at the same time.** The Israelites could not obey God and follow Moses to the Promised Land, and stay in Egypt at the same time, and though they often argued with Moses and complained about the hardships of their journey, they did finally obey the Lord, and arrived safely in Canaan.

Their journey was not a matter of forty minutes but of forty years. How did they use that time? Much of it was learning time. They left Egypt as a motley collection of slaves, a disorganised, undisciplined crowd. By the time they captured Canaan under Joshua's leadership they had become an organised nation with God's Holy Laws to guide, govern and strengthen them. Their travelling time in the wilderness had been well spent.

We can learn two major lessons from the experiences which the Hebrews had on that forty year journey: the first is that when they trusted and obeyed God, they were successful, when they were stubborn and foolish and disobeyed God, they were not successful; the second is that they learnt many lessons on the way – the journey was a series of learning experiences.

Those two major lessons are relevant to us today. Whatever journey we take: to and from school, overseas for an educational visit or a holiday, to the corner shop, or to the furthest corners of the earth, we need to trust and obey God all the way.

We also need to keep our eyes, ears and minds open and alert so that we can learn as we travel. Every journey – even the familiar journey from our homes to our school – can be a vital learning experience if we are ready to learn.

Prayer:

O great Lord, You led the Israelites safely out of slavery in Egypt and into their promised land of Canaan, lead us today in all our journeys. Help us to remember that wherever we travel You are always with us. Your love goes before us and surrounds us, and through all the many changes in our lives, You remain the same, yesterday, today and forever. Grant to us, O Lord, the faith to trust You completely on life's journey, and the courage to follow wherever Your Spirit leads us, for Jesus Christ's sake, Amen.

CHAPTER 13
The Finite and the Infinite
God and Mathematics

Scripture Reading: Genesis 15:5-7 and Numbers 1:1-4 and 47-50
Key verse: Genesis 15:5: Look now towards heaven, and tell the stars, if thou be able to number them.
Hymn: The spacious firmament on high (J. Addison, 1672–1719).

There is a possibility that someone in this audience will one day go on to study mathematics at an advanced level, then read a mathematical discipline at university and perhaps end as a professor of mathematics, or even a Nobel Prize winner. He or she may discover an important new mathematical theorem; an explanation for something that has never been satisfactorily explained before; or a way of solving a problem that has defied man's best efforts down the ages.

Finishing up as winner of mathematical honours, or lecturing in a university and writing maths text-books, may not seem very likely on days when Pythagoras' Theorem, or Venn Diagrams, or vectors, or gradients, or the binary system don't seem to make too much sense. Yet all things are possible, and we should never set our sights too low. It is only by aiming at what we really want out of life that we shall ever have any chance of achieving success. Those who care most about us – parents, church leaders, friends, teachers and relations – often have higher hopes for us than we have for ourselves. We might say as a general rule that the more people really love us, the more they desire our success and happiness. God loves us most of all, far more than the most caring parent or the truest and most devoted friend. God wants us to be happy, successful and truly fulfilled and contented. He knows us better than we know ourselves. He knows that there is something within all of us – something that He Himself has placed there – which can only find true contentment and fulfilment in Him. Even in the dullest and least imaginative human soul there is this deep longing, however hidden, for the good and the eternal things which God alone, through our Lord Jesus Christ, is able to supply.

Some of us use our mathematics at a very basic and simple level. Do you know that in remote parts of our world, even today, there are people whose language has no number greater than three? If they want to express any larger number they use another word which just means '**many**'. If a man in that place caught four fish and was asked about the extent of his catch, he would say that he had caught many

44

fish. If he had four children and was asked about the size of his family, he would say that he had many children. He would also say that there were many stars in the sky, many grains of sand on the beach, many blades of grass in the field and so on. A child of four would be many years old, and so would the oldest inhabitant of the village, who might well be in his nineties! Not being able to express numbers above three has certain serious disadvantages, but people in some parts of the world can apparently manage quite well without it!

The ancient Romans, whose Empire flourished when Jesus was on earth, conquered and administered vast territories, but they didn't know how to record 1,000,000 in the simple and easy way that we do it today by using a one followed by six zeros. If a Roman mathematician had wanted to record a million he would probably have had to write M one thousand times. We can do in three seconds what would possibly have taken him half an hour.

By the simple expedient of carrying over a number to the next column on the left every time we reach ten, using our decimal based notation, we can go on and on recording infinitely large numbers: units, tens, hundreds, then thousands and tens of thousands, and so on . . . By placing a decimal point to the right of the units, a point which divides whole numbers on the left from fractions on the right, we can use the same decimal based notation to record ever smaller and smaller numbers by adding decimal places to the right. In this way we get tenths, hundredths, thousandths, ten thousandths, and so on until we reach fractions which are infinitesimally small.

There are philosophers and theologians who would suggest to us that what we are aware of in this physical world of time and space is a shadow, or reflection, of what exists in the eternal, spiritual world. They would argue that because we are able to grapple with the idea of infinity here on earth there is a true infinity in the eternal, spiritual realm, and that Infinity – the Eternal Infinity – is just one of the numberless attributes of God our Father, whose most characteristic attribute is his Infinite Love revealed in His Son Jesus Christ.

Prayer:

Our Heavenly Father, whose power and love are infinite, help us to understand and enjoy the marvels and mysteries of the universe you have created for us to live in. Help us ever to be mindful of its heights and depths, and to think always of those who share it with us, that we, with them, may live according to your laws: in peace, in justice and in true fellowship, through Jesus Christ our Lord, Amen.

CHAPTER 14

Cause and Effect
God in the Laboratory

Scripture Reading: Mark 9:14-29

Key verse: Mark 9 verse 28: Why could not we cast him out?

Hymn: Let us with a gladsome mind, (John Milton, 1608–1674).

When we study science in the laboratory we are concerned with cause and effect. We want to know **why** certain things happen. Why does litmus turn red in the presence of an acid, or blue in the presence of an alkali? What force moves the iron filings on the paper when we hold a magnet underneath it? Why does a growing plant turn towards the light? Why does it lose its green colour if kept in the dark? We see effects and we search for causes.

Accurate observation is essential for successful scientific work. Close and careful observation and measurement by research scientists has led to many important discoveries, and will lead to many more. We can learn about causes from careful observation of effects. The cause itself is often invisible to the unaided eye. We cannot see a television signal travelling from a distant transmitter via a satellite, but we can see the effect of that signal once it reaches our television set. The invisible cause – the signal from the transmitter – produces a visible effect: light, shape, movement and colour on the screen. Because we can watch the programme we know that the signal, or a video copy of that signal, exists. The signal is the **cause** of the programme we are watching. If the signal stops for some reason – a breakdown at the transmitter, or a broken video tape – the programme on the screen stops too.

These laws of cause and effect can help to guide our thinking towards God, our Creator and our Sustainer. We cannot observe the actual signals, but we can observe their result in human lives, and from those results we can reason that the signals exist. Countless human lives have been changed for the better by coming into contact with God. These new, improved lives are the observable effects of human contact with the Great Cause. It is the loving power of God which makes these changes happen, but they will not happen until we invite God into our lives. The picture will not appear on the screen unless and until we **choose** to turn on the set.

Matthew was once a tax collector, and not a very honest one. Then Jesus called him and made him a disciple and an evangelist. Peter was an ordinary Galilean fisherman, a rather rash and impulsive character, until Jesus called him and helped him to become as strong as a rock. Saul persecuted the early church with ruthless cruelty, until his life was changed by his encounter with Jesus on the road to Damascus. John Newton was a slave trader until he was converted. The power of God made him into the Christian hymn writer who gave us "Amazing Grace".

God's redeeming love has saved alcoholics, drug addicts, criminals, thieves and gamblers and changed them into Christian citizens, evangelists, missionaries and ministers of the Gospel. It is by careful observation of those changed lives and by asking questions – as the disciples did in our Bible reading – that we can learn about God, whose redeeming love is the cause. Life itself is the great laboratory where we can learn by observation.

Prayer:

Our loving Heavenly Father, Creator and Sustainer of our universe and ourselves, we ask that you will ever keep us mindful of your Presence, so that as we learn more about all that you have made, we may be drawn ever closer to its Maker, through Jesus Christ our Lord, Amen.

CHAPTER 15

Message and Meaning
God in Language and Communication

Scripture Reading: I Kings 19:9-18

Key verse: I Kings 19 verse 13: And after the fire a still small voice.

Hymn: Hark, my soul, it is the Lord, (William Cowper, 1731–1800). (Recommended tune : Fifer's Lane by Noel Boston, 1910–1966 The English Hymnal Service Book, No. 89).

A large part of our time in school is taken up with the study of language. We learn our first language, and then proceed to use it to study other subjects. Imagine going to a school where History and Geography or Chemistry and Physics were taught in a language you had never heard before. Can you remember seeing a film made in another country, in which the actors spoke a language you did not know? You may have been able to follow some parts of it vaguely, but it wasn't the same as watching a film made in your own language.

The purpose of language is communication. Speech is really a very elaborate and complicated code made up of sounds. When people speak the same language they are really agreeing that a particular sound stands for a particular thing, or idea. When we are speaking English, we have agreed together that the sound "book" represents a number of pieces of paper, usually printed, and fastened together in a binding. If we are speaking Welsh we use "llyfr" for the same idea. In Greek we say "$\beta\iota\beta\lambda\iota\nu$ (biblion)". In Latin it is "liber".

Someone once described writing as frozen speech. The written word is the spoken word changed into visible symbols instead of audible ones. We see words instead of hearing them. But the basic idea of agreement between the writer and the reader still applies. When we read and write a language, when friends send letters, or when a great Christian leader like Paul writes to one of the early churches, the sender and the receiver must agree that certain written marks mean the same thing. This is why accurate spelling and clear legible writing are so important. They help to make our meaning clear, and they help to avoid misunderstanding and confusion.

God is the Supreme Communicator. His message is set out clearly for us in the Holy Scriptures, in the words that prophets and men of

God spoke in the past. He speaks to us most clearly, most directly, and most completely in the life, death and resurrection of our Lord Jesus Christ. God speaks today in the lives and words of those who have accepted Christ as their Saviour.

There is so **much** communication in today's highly technical world with its newspapers, its radio and TV news, cables and satellites, that we have to sort the important from the trivial, and concentrate our attention on the things that matter. The postman brings two letters. One is a leaflet advertising double glazing. The other is a letter saying that you've passed an important examination and so have a place at University. The first is trivial. The second is important. The most important communication any man or woman can ever receive in this world is God's offer of salvation through our Lord Jesus Christ.

Prayer:

Almighty and everlasting Lord, you communicate with us through your Word in the Bible, through the lives of prophets, men of God and evangelists, and most of all through the perfection of Jesus. Grant us open and receptive minds to hear your call, to understand your Word, and to live in the light of your truth and goodness, through Jesus Christ our Lord, Amen.

CHAPTER 16

Verses and Rhymes
God in Poetry

Scripture Reading: Psalm 145:1-14

Key verse: Psalm 145 verse 7: They shall abundantly utter the memory of thy great goodness, and shall sing of thy righteousness.

Hymn: Sing praise to God who reigns above, (J. J. Schutz, 1640–1690). (Translated by F. E. Cox).

When we study poetry as part of an English Literature course, or, for that matter, when we study poetry in any language, we are studying something very special and very different from ordinary prose. Poetry can be thought of as concentrated language, words under pressure. When carbon is placed under sufficient pressure it becomes a diamond. When language is pressed and moulded by the mind of a great poet, it, too, becomes the precious gem of poetry. The great J. B. Phillips, a famous translator of the Scriptures, once said that in Hebrew every letter is packed with meaning – like a tensed muscle ready to spring. So it is with poetry. The words are packed tight with meaning and feeling.

The Anglo-Saxons used to place similar sounds at the beginnings of words in their poems – what we now call alliteration. When you put similar vowel sounds close to one another like "Smooth, round boulders in a foam blue sea," we call it assonance. When the lines sound similar at the end, as they do in traditional verse, that is what we normally think of as rhyme. But Hebrew poems, particularly the Psalms and Proverbs, match **thoughts** rather than matching the sounds of the words. This is sometimes known as parallelism, and is a wonderful way of expressing the same sublime idea in two slightly different forms. Parallelism helps to emphasize and illuminate the great truths of Scripture.

If we look again at verse eight of Psalm 145, which we have just read, we find the first thought:-

The Lord is gracious and full of compassion.
This is matched perfectly against the second, parallel thought:-

Slow to anger, and of great mercy.
Think, too, of today's key verse: they shall **abundantly utter ...** that's another way of describing poetry. It is **abundant** language. It

50

radiates life and meaning in all directions. There is something wonderful inside a great poem which is demanding to be set free so that it can leap and dance from heart to heart.

People can be like poems. We can experience that same inner power, if we let Christ into our lives and live with God's Laws as our guiding principles.

There is as much difference between the Christ-centred life and the self-centred life, as there is between reading a great poem and reading an out of date telephone directory.

Prayer:

Dear Lord and Father, help us to be so aware of your presence, your love, and your care for us, that we feel the gratitude and praise which the psalmist felt of old. Help us to fill our lives with purpose and meaning, so that each day becomes a glorious adventure for Christ. Give us good thoughts to think and faithful words to say, for the sake of Him who loved us to the Cross and beyond, Jesus Christ our Lord, Amen.

CHAPTER 17

Knowing when to Stop
God in Punctuation

Scripture Reading: Job 38:1-12

Key verse: Job 38 verse 11: Hitherto shalt thou come, but no further: and here shall thy proud waves be stayed.

Hymn: Thou whose almighty Word, (J. Marriott, 1780 –1825).

Some years ago a well-known manufacturer of brake linings for cars advertised with the slogan: **Never start something you can't stop!** There's an old children's story about a magic mill that would grind anything you asked for. It was taken from its rightful owner by someone who knew the magic word to start it, but who didn't know how to stop it. Wanting some salt on his food when on board ship, he ordered the mill to grind salt. As it was impossible to stop it, the sailors threw it overboard before the weight of the salt sank their ship – which, according to the story, explains why the seas are salty!

A flow of good ideas is very useful for an English student writing essays, or compositions. Authors and public speakers hate to "dry up" – to reach a point where their ideas cease to flow. But knowing when to stop is just as important as knowing when to start and how to proceed once we've started.

A writer who fails to punctuate his work makes the reader's task almost impossible. All kinds of curious and comical errors creep into our writing if the punctuation is missing, or in the wrong places. One of the most famous of these examples is the missing full stop in the historical statement about King Charles I. "The King walked and talked half an hour after his head was cut off." The missing full stop should, of course, go in after **talked**, so that the statement really reads:

"The King walked and talked. Half an hour after his head was cut off." The unusual use of **after**, when **later** would clarify the meaning, also adds to the confusion.

There are many things which are good at their best, and harmless at their worst, **provided that we know when to stop.** A joke, or a little gentle teasing, may do no harm **once**, but if it is persisted in it becomes cruel. Food, at the right time and in the right quantities, is good for us, but we have to know when to stop. Dieting, if we are seriously overweight, may be beneficial, but, if it becomes an obsession, it can lead to very serious medical problems like **anorexia nervosa.** The abuse of alcohol, solvents and drugs, provides terrible examples of what can happen to people when they get into situations which they can't stop. Scripture tells us how God our Creator and Sustainer has set limits and boundaries to seas and lands. We should learn from this example in the earth itself to set proper limits and boundaries in our own lives.

Prayer:

O God, our Father, Creator and Sustainer of the universe, You have set proper limits and boundaries for all things. Help us, Lord, to see and understand the limits and boundaries You have set for us, and, as our Lord Jesus Christ withstood temptation for our sakes, help us to withstand temptation for His sake, who loved us and gave His life for us, Amen.

CHAPTER 18

Addition and Subtraction
God in Computation

Scripture Reading: Luke 2:1-4

Key verse: Luke 2 verse 1: There went out a decree from Caesar Augustus, that all the world should be taxed.

Hymn: Teach me, my God and King, (G. Herbert, 1593–1633).

Scarcely an hour passes when we do not need to count something, or to perform a simple addition or subtraction. How many pencils were given out? How many pens, or coins, or sweets, did I have in that pocket? How many dinner tickets have I got left? If I spend x amount of money on this item, will I have enough left to pay my bus fare home? If I'm playing chess can I afford to exchange the knight for two pawns? I've already spent too long on the first question in this examination. How many minutes should I allocate to questions four and five? How many books in the whole Bible? Sixty-six. How can I remember that? There are thirty-nine in the Old Testament and twenty-seven in the New Testament. If I take the three and multiply it by the nine, I get twenty-seven. Then I add thirty-nine to twenty-seven to obtain the answer sixty-six. We use numbers so often, and in so many ways.

Most of our daily computation takes this basic form of adding and subtracting. The other two common processes – multiplying and dividing – can be thought of as quick methods of adding and subtracting in special cases. If we add five and five and five we get fifteen. If we say three **times** five instead, we also get fifteen. If we added five to itself twenty times instead of three times we should, of course, get 100. Twenty separate small additions would be very tedious, and we find the multiplication process useful in cases like this. Division is a form of repeated subtraction. We do not ask: how many times can I take five away from 100? We ask instead: how many times does five go into 100? Again, twenty small, separate subtractions would be very tedious and time consuming. Division is a helpful process, too.

So then, for most ordinary, everyday computations we need only the four rules of basic arithmetic: addition and multiplication, subtraction and division.

Just as those four rules will help us with life's basic number situations, so there are four spiritual rules which will help us with the far more important moral, ethical and behavioural situations which we encounter every day.

The first rule is this. Will what I am planning to do **add** anything to the world's supply of goodness and happiness? Who will be better off if I do it? Who will be helped by it? Will God be praised or glorified, if I do this? If the answer is "Yes", if what we are planning **will** add something good to life, something of which God will approve, then let us do it.

The subtraction rule asks a similar question. Will what I am proposing to do take away a burden from someone else? Will it reduce the world's sorrow and distress in any way? Will God approve of it? If the answer is yes – then let us do it.

In the same way we can ask whether something good may increase, or multiply, because of what we are hoping to do. And we can also ask whether, by taking on part of someone else's burden, we can share or divide that burden with him. There are four rules for basic computation and four rules for basic living.

Prayer

O loving Lord, You order and rule the universe, grant us Your help to order and rule our lives. Teach us that it is better to give than to receive, better to help than to judge or criticise, better to love than to hate. Help us always to try to add to the world's goodness and to reduce its evil and sorrow, for the sake of Him who redeemed us, Jesus Christ our Lord, Amen.

CHAPTER 19

Finishing Things Properly
God in Completion and Fulfilment

Scripture Reading: John 17:1-8

Key verse: John 17 verse 4: I have finished the work which thou gavest me to do.

Hymn: O Jesus, I have promised, (J. E. Bode, 1816–1874).

Many an examination mark has been lower than a candidate really could have obtained simply because a question begun well was not finished. Perhaps the candidate ran out of time or ideas. Perhaps, he, or she, was too anxious to get on to another question.

How many times has a teacher said to you, or written on some half-completed exercise, "Please get this finished"? In craft work particularly, it is very important to finish things off properly: the final cleaning and polishing stages, the putting away of materials, implements and equipment. All the good work and hard effort that have gone into the early stage of learning or creating will largely be wasted unless we finish well.

How true this is in sports and games! In a long distance race two or three strong competitors have run neck and neck for miles, keeping up a fast pace, making tremendous efforts to hold on. The winner will be the man or woman who can finish the race best, who can bring out that little **extra** burst of energy and determination right at the end.

After studying a subject for years in school, it is the effort we make with our revision, in those vital months and weeks leading up to our examinations, which counts for so much. Without it, the earlier years of learning and preparation will be thrown away.

Bede was a famous theologian and historian, who lived and worked at Jarrow from 672–735. He was very concerned to finish the book he was working on – his translation of John's Gospel – before he died. The quiet but determined and saintly monk did manage to finish it, in spite of his physical weakness. He knew the importance of completing things well.

In the Parable of the Sower, which our Lord Himself told, we hear how some of the seed – the Word of God – fell on a rock and withered away almost as soon as it sprang up because it lacked moisture. Jesus explained that this represented those who heard God's Word and received it enthusiastically at first, but because they had "no root" in themselves, they soon gave up the faith when there were persecutions or hardships. In other words, they lacked staying power and finishing power.

It is good to begin well. It is better to go on well. It is best and most important of all to finish well. Jesus Himself, as He completed the work of redemption on the cross said, "It is finished." He, above all others, knew how to see things through to the end.

Prayer:

Great heavenly Father, You know our every failing and our every weakness. You know how often we feel tempted to give up some good work because it has become difficult. You know how easily we abandon our good intentions when we find them hard to fulful. Grant us that strength of purpose and unbreakable resolve which was in Christ Jesus our Lord, that we may strive as He strove, and so complete our work for You. We ask it in the Name of Him who completed the work of salvation for us, Jesus Christ our Lord, Amen.

CHAPTER 20

Money and Value
God in Economics

Scripture Reading: Luke 16:13, 19-26

Key verse: Luke 16 verse 13: Ye cannot serve God and mammon.

Hymn: Jesus calls us! – o'er the tumult, (Mrs C. F. Alexander, 1818–1895).

Those of us who are studying economics as an examination subject in its own right, or who have looked at economic factors in history and geography, will know that economics is sometimes referred to as "the science of wealth". There is no shortage of economic material to study in the world around us. Our papers, radio and television programmes are packed with economic news, statistics and forecasts. Almost every journalist and politician is an amateur economist, and the fact that they very rarely agree with one another, and that many of their predictions are inaccurate anyway, does not seem to discourage them. Most people are interested in money. Some are fascinated by it. Some are obsessed and possessed by it. It is so powerful and dominant in our society that it is very difficult for any of us not to get it out of proportion. Yet Jesus teaches us over and over again that we must not allow it to dominate our lives or distract us from our real, eternal, spiritual objectives.

He makes it clear in the Parable of Dives, the rich man, and Lazarus, the beggar, that wealth has harmed the rich man far more than poverty has harmed Lazarus. Jesus also told the Parable of the Rich Fool, the man who was a very prosperous farmer. He was planning to pull down his barns and build bigger ones to store his corn and other produce, and then to relax and enjoy himself for years. **He died that same night.** His foolishness lay in regarding the things of this world, and his material prosperity, as being important. Compared to the spiritual and eternal values, they are of no importance at all.

Of course we all have to deal with economic situations in our daily lives. Of course it affects us when prices rise faster than incomes. Of course we are concerned about sickness and unemployment. Jesus Himself lived in the ordinary world of everyday life in a province of the Roman Empire. He knew all about the economic difficulties which ordinary people faced every day. But He also knew the difference between what was important and eternal, and what was worldly, temporal and trivial. King Herod lived in a luxurious palace. John the Baptist lived a hard, rough, outdoor life in the wilderness. He had very few of this world's goods, yet he was incomparably richer than Herod in the things that really mattered.

A Christian economist should ask himself this question. How can the world's wealth best be used to glorify God and to help those in need to live happier and fuller lives? We are all stewards, responsible to God. We have no material possessions when we enter this earthly life, and we take none of our possessions with us when we leave it. God does not judge our economic record by whether we are rich or poor, but by what we **do** with whatever wealth we have.

Prayer:

Lord, help us to remember that the things of this world last only for a short time, but Your Kingdom lasts forever. Help us always to value honesty and integrity more than personal gain. Help us to honour You and Your Law in all our earning and spending, and in all our buying and selling. Make us good and faithful stewards of all that You provide for us. Help us to be generous to those in need, as You are generous to all mankind. We ask it in the name of Jesus Christ our Lord, who gave everything for us. Amen.

CHAPTER 21

Seeing and Observing
God on our Blind Spot

Scripture Reading: 1 Corinthians 13:1-13

Key verse: 1 Corinthians 13 verse 12: But then I shall know even as also I am known.

Hymn: Loving Shepherd of thy sheep, (Jane E. Leeson, 1807–1892).

Sometimes we experience a kind of sportsman's blind spot when we are playing tennis, badminton or cricket. You **think** that you are about to make contact, but you don't. It was almost as if a mysterious hole had appeared in the middle of the bat or the centre of the racquet.

Blind spots are very dangerous when we're walking, cycling or driving. We need to look very carefully in all directions and to keep alert when using the roads. When a car is **just** behind you in the inside or outside lane, and you may not be able to hear its engine clearly because of heavy traffic, it is on your "blind spot" and very dangerous.

Imaginative chess players, who rely on flair rather than carefully memorised openings and defences, will sometimes work out strong and complex plans five or six moves ahead, only to overlook one tiny detail and lose a major piece because of that blind spot.

In Greek mythology, the mighty hero Achilles was invulnerable except for one heel. After many great battles and other exploits, including his victory over Hector, the Trojan champion, Achilles died as the result of an arrow in his unprotected heel. It was his blind spot, his fatal weakness.

Most of us have blind spots when it comes to being aware of our own faults. Our vision is all too sharp when we look at the faults of others – in fact we usually magnify them. Jesus knew this very well, and warned us against it in the parable of the speck of dust and the plank of wood. There are people whose spiritual vision is almost totally obstructed by the plank of their own sin. Nevertheless they enthusiastically offer to remove the tiny speck of sin which they claim to see in the spiritual eye of someone else!

The great Scots poet, Robert Burns, longed for the ability to see himself as others saw him, and all of us would benefit from a clear, honest look at ourselves. As we read in Paul's letter to the Corinthians, the day will come when we shall know even as we are known. There will be no hiding place for our blind spots in the Eternal Light of Heaven.

Prayer:

O God our Father, source of all truth and fountain of all understanding, grant us the wisdom and courage to look honestly into our own lives, to see our faults and to bring them to You to be cleared away. Help us to judge ourselves strictly, and to judge others mercifully, with understanding and compassion. May our Lord Jesus Christ, who gave sight to the blind, give spiritual sight to us, that we may always walk in His ways, for His Name's sake, Amen.

CHAPTER 22

Test-tubes and Chemicals
God in Synthesis and Analysis

Scripture Reading: 1 Samuel 16:4-12

Key verse: 1 Samuel 16 verse 12: This is he.

Hymn: O worship the King, (R. Grant, 1779–1838).

Dictionaries define chemistry as the science of the elements and compounds, and their laws of combination and change resulting from interaction between substances in contact. Chemists are interested in what happens when something burns and its hydrogen combines with oxygen to form water, while its carbon combines with oxygen to form carbon dioxide. Chemists are interested in what happens when an electric current passes through water and breaks it down into the basic gases : hydrogen and oxygen. When something combines with something else to form a more complicated compound, we call it **synthesis.** When compounds are broken down into simpler forms we call it **analysis. Synthesizing** is building up, or bringing things together. **Analysing** is separating out, or taking things apart to see what they're made of. In chemistry we study both processes.

In the passage of Scripture which we have just read, Samuel was searching for the man whom the Lord had told him to anoint as king. He discarded one possibility after another until the Lord told him that he had found the right man. In some examinations and tests in chemistry, the candidate is given a sample of liquid, or powder, and asked to analyse it, to find out what's in it, or to identify the substance. A chemical analyst will apply one test after another, rejecting each idea in turn if it does not meet the requirements of the test, until he discovers what the substance is.

In wartime, when there are often serious shortages, chemists will find ways of synthesizing artificial substitutes. Cloth made from nylon, rayon or other man-made chemical fibres is said to be **synthetic,** whereas cotton, wool and linen are natural fibres. Very few commercially produced drinks labelled **lemonade** have ever seen a real, natural lemon. Their flavouring is synthetic.

In the spiritual world, we can also observe these processes of synthesis and analysis as men and women come into contact with

Christ. Their pride and vanity, their weakness and selfishness, their cowardice and aggression are changed or broken down, and good things are synthesized in their places. Pride becomes determination. Vanity becomes a striving to be the best one can be for Christ. Weakness becomes strength. Selfishness evaporates and is replaced by a love for the Lord and for others. Cowardice becomes courage, and aggression is directed against evil.

Prayer:

O loving Father, come into our lives and improve them. Help us to break down and change all that spoils our lives. Rid us of all that is not worthy. Help us to build up those parts of our lives which are acceptable to You. Help us to test every word and every deed against the perfect standard of Your Purity, that, day by day, we may, with Christ's help, become more like Him, for His Name's sake, Amen.

CHAPTER 23

Nature and Living Things
God in Biology

Scripture Reading: Job 38:39 - 39:8

Key verse: Job 38:41: Who provideth for the Raven his food?

Hymn: All creatures of our God and King, (W. H. Draper, 1855–1933).

Biologists very often ask the same questions which God asked Job in our Scripture reading. We want to know about the feeding habits of different birds and animals. We want to find out where they live and what they do. We are becoming increasingly aware today of the interdependence of human beings and animal and plant life. Many of our industrial processes have already affected rivers, lakes and oceans. The safe disposal of waste, particularly toxic and nuclear waste, causes grave concern. The siting of nuclear power stations and the problems of radiation leakage are very much in people's minds. Lead from car exhausts, and the products of combustion from industry cause vast ecological problems. We are becoming more and more aware of the need for care and conservation. Endangered species of animals – such as the whale – urgently need our care and protection. Fishing grounds are in danger of being over-fished. Insecticide sprays and artificial fertilizers can kill wild life and create serious health problems for human beings. The more we know about biology, about **how** nature works, the better we can hope to protect the other living things that share our world with us.

Many of our Lord's parables and teachings were based on nature and natural processes, and we can learn a great many spiritual truths by observing Nature.

Nature has its cycles and seasons. After the seemingly cold, bleak and lifeless period of Winter, the resurrection message of Spring bursts out with every new bud and leaf. Just as Nature lives again, so shall we. We watch a tiny baby bird struggling awkwardly out of its eggshell, and know that one day those comical miniature wings will spread with strength and grace to carry it effortlessly across the sky. The newly converted Christian often struggles awkwardly at first, but God's Love and the indwelling Power of Christ will one day enable that awkward new Christian to soar to great spiritual heights.

Prayer:

Lord of all life, help us to understand our part in Your Creation and to be in harmony with Your Will for us and for all living things. Teach us to respect, to love and to care for all life, and to learn of You from what You have created. For the sake of Jesus Christ our Lord, Amen.

CHAPTER 24

Managing and Delegating
God in Organisation

Scripture Reading: Exodus 18:13-26

Key verse: Exodus 18 verse 25: And Moses chose able men, and made them heads over the people.

Hymn: Help us to help each other, Lord, (Charles Wesley, 1707–1788).

In the passage of Scripture that we have just read, we see a very clear example of the kind of management problem that affects organisations today. Moses, the man God had chosen to lead His people out of slavery in Egypt, was involved with them from early morning until late at night. He was judging every dispute himself. He was personally advising everyone who came to him for guidance and help: and there were thousands upon thousands of Israelites who needed him.

When we get into the kind of management situation which Moses was in, it's not good for the manager and it's not good for the people he's looking after. The stress and strain begins to tell. After a time the manager's judgements and decisions deteriorate because he's exhausted and over-worked. A man in the situation Moses was in can't always see an answer to his own difficulties because he's too close to the problem. He's too involved in actually doing things to have the time to think about how to do them better.

He needs an adviser to observe the problems from outside, and think about ways to solve them. When Moses first left Egypt after killing the Egyptian task-master who was ill-treating a Hebrew slave, Moses had found sanctuary in the land of Midian. There he had married Zipporah, daughter of Jethro, the priest of Midian. Years later, after Moses had led the Israelites to freedom, his father-in-law, Jethro, came to visit him in the wilderness.

The wise old Midianite priest watched Moses at work judging and counselling vast numbers of Israelites all through a long, weary day. Jethro was the observer and adviser that Moses needed to help him with his management problem. As a result of Jethro's advice, Moses set up a system by which the work he had been doing himself could be delegated to other leaders: rulers of thousands, rulers of hundreds, rulers of fifties and rulers of tens. These men dealt with all the minor problems, and referred only the major problems up to Moses.

Every school has systems of delegation. Deputy Heads and Senior Teachers carry out special jobs to help the Head. One will be responsible for the time-table; another will look after school visits; one may be in charge of pupils' welfare; another will be responsible for furniture, premises and equipment. Someone else will lead a team of curriculum developers. If a Senior Teacher has charge of all school visits for the Head, another member of staff will take responsibility for one particular visit. So organisers and managers help one another at different levels. If the whole organisation is to work properly, everyone must fulfil his or her responsibilities conscientiously. Whatever our task is, we must take pride in doing it to the best of our ability. Whether we are a team member or a team leader, whether we are in charge of ten or in charge of 1,000, we have a duty to God and to ourselves to do our best at all times.

Prayer:

O God, the Leader and Father of us all, help us to manage and organise our lives. Help us to respect and trust others so that we may learn to delegate some tasks. Help others to trust and respect us, so that they can come to rely upon us to do our duty faithfully. Help us to understand our place in the team, and to work harmoniously with others for the good of all. We ask it in the Name of the Greatest Leader, who called His disciples not servants, but friends, Jesus Christ our Lord, Amen.

CHAPTER 25

Options and Choices
God in the Curriculum

Scripture Reading: Joshua 24:14-18

Key verse: Joshua 24 verse 15: Choose you this day whom ye will serve.

Hymn: I bind unto myself today, (Patrick of Ireland, 372–466). (Translated by Mrs C. F. Alexander 1818–1895).

One of the most precious and, at the same time, the most perilous of gifts bestowed on human beings is our freedom to choose. God gives us life. God gives us the power to think for ourselves, and God gives us choice, or freewill. Because God Himself is love, and because love and freedom are inseparable, if we cannot choose we cannot love.

If in some science fiction story, a robot or android was programmed to love the scientist who had created it, what kind of love would it be? In Shakespeare's famous comedy "A Midsummer Night's Dream" much of the plot depends upon a magic spell which makes the victim fall in love with the first person he, or she, sees after the spell has been cast. What kind of love is that? For a brief period after it has hatched, a baby duckling's mind is programmed to follow the first moving object it sees. Normally this is the mother duck, and all is well for the duckling. But in certain biological experiments ducklings have been programmed artificially to follow such unlikely and unhelpful "substitute mothers" as pieces of coloured cloth or even a broom! These unfortunate ducklings had their choices made for them by the experimenter. What sort of love could there have been between the duckling and the piece of cloth?

Without true freedom, there can be no true love.

Time is a scarce and precious resource for everyone. We have to choose how we will use it. When we are planning a school curriculum – which subjects will be offered for students to learn – we realise just what a precious commodity time is. Everything we do has its opportunity cost because we cannot learn two things simultaneously. If we are studying English on Tuesday afternoon, second lesson, we cannot study mathematics during that same period. The opportunity cost of the English is mathematics, and the opportunity cost of the mathematics is English.

In many senior schools, students have to choose their options at the end of their third year. It may not be possible to study history **and** chemistry. It may not be possible to take both geography **and** physics. We are called upon to choose, and every choice has its opportunity cost.

When we make important choices such as subject options we are able to ask teachers and parents for their advice. In our Scripture reading today, we heard how the Israelites were faced with the most important choice of all – whether to worship the Lord, or to worship idols. Joshua, their leader, gave them his advice. He told them what his choice was: "As for me and my house, we will serve the Lord."

Prayer:

O loving heavenly Father, You have given us the power to choose. You have given us the freedom to accept or to reject Your Love. Grant us the wisdom to make the right decisions. We thank You for this great and precious gift of freedom, and we offer it to You again, as we ask for Your guidance and help in every choice we are called upon to make. We ask these prayers in the name of Jesus our Lord, who chose to come to earth in the form of a man, and to die for our salvation, Amen.

CHAPTER 26

Designing, Cutting and Sewing
God in Needlecraft

Scripture Reading: Matthew 9:10-17

Key verse: Matthew 9 verse 16: No man putteth a piece of new cloth unto an old garment.

Hymn: Jerusalem the golden, (Bernard of Cluny, 12th Century).
(Translated by John Mason Neale, 1818–1866).

In order to understand our Lord's parable about the new cloth being used as a patch on an old garment, we have to remember that in first century Palestine, the new cloth would not have been pre-shrunk. Such new cloth, used over old cloth which had already shrunk, would tear the old garment when the new patch shrunk. The resulting damage would be worse than the original hole.

Jesus was pointing out that the new, God-filled life, which followed contact with Him, could not be merely a patch over the old life. The new Christian way of life which Jesus offered was no mere patch to cover over the shortcomings of the existing system. Becoming a Christian means making a complete break with sin and worldly things, and starting an exciting new life with Christ.

As we think about our Lord's teaching about this new and old cloth, so we are reminded of needlecraft lessons in school. Garments are designed in needlecraft lessons with a view to their style, fashion, suitability and function. A fisherman's jersey and a football supporter's scarf serve very different purposes. A protective apron for cooking and washing up represents a completely different concept from a decorative summer dress. Each has its own set of criteria for success. The apron is expected to be strong, protective and durable. The dress is expected to look attractive.

Given the right design, there follows the choice of suitable fabrics, colours and patterns. Once materials are chosen and cut to shape they have to be joined together, sewn neatly and sewn strongly. Every fabric has its own advantages and disadvantages: wool, cotton, linen, nylon, velvet, lace and brocade – all offer different qualities to the garment maker. The various methods of seaming and stitching also have their special advantages and disadvantages. The successfully finished garment is the end product of many careful and skilful choices by the garment maker.

Starting a Christian life is not trying to patch up our old bad habits. Starting a Christian life is a whole fresh undertaking – making something quite new. Just as we begin designing a garment by asking about the purpose of that garment, so we should begin our new life in Christ by asking God what His purpose is for us. The purpose of the Christian life is to praise and glorify God and to help others for His sake, to enjoy fellowship with God and our brothers and sisters in Christ forever. Just as our needlecraft teacher will help us to make a successful garment from thread, needle and cloth, so God will help us to make a living garment from thoughts, words and deeds dedicated to Him.

Prayer:

O God our Father, whose Son, our Lord Jesus Christ, taught in parables, teach us to make the best of our lives. Help us to understand that life with Christ is a new and wonderful experience, not just a patching of what is old. Help us to understand Your will for us, and to join our thoughts, words and deeds into a living garment of prayer, praise and service, for the sake of Him whose life was more perfect than the seamless robe He wore, Jesus Christ our Lord, Amen.

CHAPTER 27

Moulding and Forming
God in the Potter's Clay

Scripture Reading: Jeremiah 18:1-6

Key verse: Jeremiah 18 verse 6: Behold, as the clay is in the potter's hand, so are ye in my hand.

Hymn: Take my life, and let it be, (Frances Ridley Havergal, 1836–1879).

When you make something from clay in a pottery lesson as part of your art and craft work, you are using a skill that is thousands of years old. Like the shuttle and the loom, the potter's wheel has a very long history. Prophets like Jeremiah – men of great spiritual insight – could readily see the similarity between the potter fashioning his clay and God fashioning His universe and the events taking place within it. Those of you who have already done some pottery will know just how difficult it is to turn the wet and formless clay into something useful and beautiful. Now try to imagine that the clay upon which you were working was alive and intelligent, and could – within the limits of its nature – decide to co-operate with the potter or to try to go its own way. Imagine also that this living, intelligent clay is of such a nature that it can only be truly happy when it has been fashioned into good, beautiful and useful things. The potter loves the clay, knows what is best for it, and wants what is best for it. Only by co-operating with the potter can the clay fulfil its rightful destiny, but because the clay has a will of its own, it often chooses wrongly. It spoils the good design the potter has for it by its own wilfulness and stubbornness. But, as we read in Jeremiah, even an earthly potter is not defeated when the vessel is marred. He makes a new vessel from that same clay.

God has made each one of us as a separate individual with a unique personality and characteristics. He loves and cares for each of us with a love that is unimaginably stronger than any love we can either give or receive here on earth. He loves the most selfish person more than that person loves himself. God knows us far better than we can ever know ourselves. His plan for us – if only we will agree to let Him carry it out – will make us far happier than anything we think we can plan for ourselves. If we, the living clay, will only trust the Divine Potter and give our lives to Him, He will do incomparably more for us than we can begin to imagine at this time.

However much we may already have marred the clay of our lives, by our sin, stupidity and selfishness, God can still take them over and put them right. The same Jeremiah who wrote with such insight about the potter also wrote that God has said, "Behold I am the Lord, the God of all flesh: is there any thing too hard for me?" There are few things harder than putting right a human life that has gone wrong because of sin. Jesus went all the way to Calvary to do it, but, as Jeremiah has shown us, nothing is too hard for God.

Prayer:

All loving, creating and sustaining Father, we come before You now, conscious of our sin, our weakness and our human failure. We know that much that is wrong in our lives is the result of our own sin, our own foolishness, our own selfishness and wrong-doing. We would ask you, Lord, to take over our lives, and to re-make us after the likeness of Your Son, Jesus Christ the Righteous, in whose Name we ask this and every prayer, Amen.

CHAPTER 28

Presence and Absence
God in Registration

Scripture Reading: Revelation 3:1-8

Key verse: Revelation 3 verse 5: I will not blot out his name out of the book of life.

Hymn: When the trumpet of the Lord shall sound, (J. M. Black)
(In "Sacred Songs and Solos" compiled by Ira D. Sankey).

Registration is a regular fixed point in every school's routine. Each morning and afternoon the roll is duly called. Attendances and absences are recorded. Totals and percentages are calculated. The necessary steps are taken to improve unsatisfactory attendance and poor punctuality. When pupils leave the area their names are taken off the register of their old school and added to the register at their new school. When students change classes, their names are transferred from one register to another.

Registration procedures apply when patients attend their doctor's or dentist's surgeries, when soldiers take part in roll call on parade, or when voters are listed as being eligible for an election. The clerk of the court calls out the names of jurors as they enter the jury box before being sworn in or affirming.

After important university degree examinations lists of successful candidates are published by the university. There are medical registers showing who is allowed to practise medicine, and legal registers of qualified barristers and solicitors. There is a publication called **"Who's Who"** listing the names of people who – at least in the editor's opinion – are sufficiently famous and important to be included. And, of course, we have all heard of the **"Guinness Book of Records"** which lists all kinds of things – some of them rather curious – for which people hold a world record.

It is very important for students to attend school regularly and punctually. School registers are, therefore, important documents. Military, medical and professional registers are also important. It is decidedly arguable whether inclusion in a list of the allegedly famous by this world's standards is of any importance at all, but perhaps most of us are vulnerable to the temptations of vanity from time to time!

There is one list however, one register, which is of absolute importance. It is the one book in which we have to be quite certain that our names have been included. That book is the Book of Life, which we read about in today's portion of the Scriptures. There is only one way to get our names into that book, and that is to believe sincerely in the Lord Jesus Christ and trust in His redeeming power for our eternal salvation. We cannot get included simply by attending some Church or Chapel. We cannot pass difficult qualifying examinations like doctors, or lawyers, and be included that way. We cannot enlist like soldiers and be included on a military roll. It is faith in Christ alone that enters a name in that book.

Prayer:

O Lord God, we know You sent Your Son Jesus Christ to die on Calvary for our salvation. Help us to understand and accept that Great Work which He undertook for us and all mankind. Help us so to think about His Incarnation, His Life of Ministry on earth, His Sufferings and Death, His Resurrection and Ascension, that we may truly believe on Him and live as His followers, that our names may be written forever in His Book of Life, for His Name's sake, Amen.

CHAPTER 29

Extracting the Essentials
God in Précis and Summary

Scripture Reading: Matthew 22:31-40

Key verse: Matthew 22 verse 40: On these two commandments hang all the law and the prophets.

Hymn: Lord, Thy Word abideth, (H. W. Baker, 1821–1877).

There are several ways in which English examiners can test a candidate's knowledge of the language, and his or her ability to use it. There are multiple choice answer sheets – very convenient for marking by computer – in which the candidate is presented with five or six possible answers and asked to mark the one which he or she thinks is correct. There is essay or composition writing : here the examiner is looking for the candidate's ability to write clearly, imaginatively and relevantly around an essay theme or title. Some essays ask for descriptive powers, others for narrative talent. Some require accurate, factual descriptions of techniques or processes, others look for philosophical abstractions. Some even give a candidate the opportunity to write a poem on the given theme or subject.

There are comprehension questions: the candidate is given a passage to read and then asked questions about what he has read. There are questions which ask the candidate to give the precise meaning of some word or phrase as used in the passage. Then there are précis or summary questions. Here the candidate is given quite a lengthy passage and told to reduce its length by about two-thirds while retaining all the important information which it contains. When we listen to a news bulletin we are getting the main facts in a shortened form. This is a summary, or précis, of the news.

During one of His many conflicts with the hypocritical Scribes, Pharisees and Sadducees, Jesus was asked which was the greatest commandment, as we heard in today's Scripture reading. He replied that the First Commandment was to love God wholeheartedly and unreservedly, and the Second Commandment was to love our neighbours as ourselves. He said that all the sacred law and the writings of the prophets hung on those two Great Commandments. Those words of our Lord Jesus are the greatest and most effective précis of all time. They completely encapsulate the Divine Law together with the Divine Intention behind that law.

When we examine the Ten Commandments we find that the underlying principle behind each one is either to honour and serve God, or to treat our fellow beings as we ourselves would wish to be treated by them. When we study the justice of Amos or the mercy and forgiveness of Hosea, we find these two great principles – love to God and man – expanded yet again.

Next time we are confronted by a précis or summary question in an examination, let us remember again, the Great Précis which Jesus created: putting God first and loving others as we love ourselves is the eternal truth on which all law and all prophecy hang.

Prayer:

O Lord our God, You are the First, and the Last, the Essential of all Essentials. Help us always to distinguish between what is necessary and important to our spiritual development, and what is trivial, worldly and of no consequence. May we always remember and act upon the commandments of our Lord Jesus Christ to love You with all our heart, mind and strength, and to love our neighbours as ourselves, for the sake of Him who loved us and gave His Life for us, Jesus Christ our Lord, Amen.

CHAPTER 30

Remedial Education
God in our Difficulties

Scripture Reading: Exodus 14:5-14

Key verse: Exodus 14 verse 13: Fear ye not, stand still and see the salvation of the Lord.

Hymn: Oft in danger, oft in woe, (H. Kirke White, 1785 –1806). (Francis S. Fuller-Maitland, 1809–1877, and others).

Many years ago, the author of this book was teaching a pupil whom we will identify only by his Christian name of Neil. If he ever reads this page, he will recognize himself immediately, and the author hopes that he does, for this story is a tribute to him.

Neil was a very pleasant, hard-working lad, but he had great difficulty in learning to read. Some people do. There are many excellent people, with strong characters and much ability in other directions who just find reading difficult. Even as a teenager, Neil was struggling with words that most of us learn to read at junior school. The author used to have sandwiches in his classroom at lunch-times in those days, and during those lunch-hours Neil would practise his reading. When a word was new or difficult, Neil would be gently prompted. One day, as he struggled over a word that was causing him particular problems, Neil crashed his fist down on the desk and said through gritted teeth, "I'm **never** going to give up! I **will** get it!" And he did. It took him longer than it takes most people, but he was a competent reader by the time he left school. The author has always admired Neil, and will never forget him. He still uses the example of Neil's courage and determination in his own assemblies.

In every school there are boys and girls who have problems like Neil's. These problems are not their fault in any way. There are a few very fortunate people to whom academic work is extremely easy. There are some less fortunate people – like Neil – to whom academic work is very hard indeed. Most of us fall somewhere between those two extremes. There is no particular merit in achieving something which comes easily to us. The merit lies in overcoming difficulties, however hard they are, and in **never** giving up. It is a far greater achievement for a boy or girl with a learning handicap to struggle to read a few hundred words, than it is for a very gifted academic pupil to pass all his or her public examinations at Grade A. Sometimes, like the Israelites trapped between Pharaoh and the Red Sea, we can see no way out of our difficulties. It is then that we must be more determined than ever and say to ourselves, as Moses of old said to the Israelites: "Fear ye not, stand still and see the salvation of the Lord."

Prayer:

O Lord, our loving heavenly Father, be with us all the days of our life and see us safely through the problems and difficulties that we encounter. Be with us as You were with Moses and the Israelites of old when Pharaoh pursued them to the Red Sea. Grant us enough determination, faith and courage never to give up, and give us the grace to trust in Your deliverance once we have done all that we can do for ourselves. We ask it in the name of Him who persevered in all things, even death, for our sakes, Jesus Christ our Lord, Amen.

CHAPTER 31

Acting a Part
God in Plays and Drama

Scripture Reading: Genesis 27:15-25
Key verse: Genesis 27 verse 18: Who art thou, my son?
Hymn: Just as I am, without one plea, (Charlotte Elliott, 1789–1871).

In our Scripture reading we have just heard how Rebekah and Jacob deceived Isaac, and cheated Esau out of his old father's blessing. It was not difficult to carry out the deception because old Isaac was practically blind, and he could only distinquish between his sons – Esau and Jacob – by listening to their voices and by touching their hands. Jacob was disguised. He was acting the part of his brother, and, although Isaac had some doubts at first, Jacob's deception succeeded. Not many years afterwards, Jacob was deceived. He loved Rachel, and worked for seven years without payment in order to pay the "bride price" which her father demanded. At the ceremony, the bride was heavily veiled, and it was not until the service was over that Jacob realised he had married Rachel's elder sister, Leah. Her father had deceived him. Leah had acted her sister's part at the wedding. When King Saul was losing battles against the Philistines, and things were going very badly for him, he went to consult a medium, a woman known as the Witch of Endor. Saul had himself passed laws forbidding magic and the calling up of the spirits of the dead. Now he wanted to consult the spirit of the prophet Samuel. He hoped that Samuel would advise and help him in his war against the Philistines. Saul disguised himself when he went to Endor, but his conversation with the spirit of Samuel soon revealed his true identity to the terrified medium. Saul had not acted his part very successfully, and the only word which Samuel had for him was stern warning of the disaster to come.

In I Kings 14 we read how King Jeroboam sent his wife in disguise to consult the prophet Ahijah at Shiloh, but the Lord had revealed her true identity to the prophet even before she arrived.

When King Ahab was fighting against Benhadad of Syria, the Syrian war leaders had been instructed to seek out Ahab on the battlefield and destroy him. But Ahab had disguised himself and given his conspicuous royal robes to his ally, King Jehoshaphat of Judah. In spite of Ahab's attempted deception he was mortally wounded in the battle, but Jehoshaphat came through alive.

Many years ago, Thurber, the great American humorist, wrote a story about Walter Mitty, rather a weak and ineffective character who day-dreamed about being a super-hero. The story was later made into an excellent film, starring Danny Kaye. Some of you may have seen it on television. Walter Mitty acted out great adventures in his mind to compensate for the drab ordinariness and frustration of his daily life.

There have been several real Walter Mitty types recently, who have pretended to be someone important, and have got away with the deception for a while because they were skilful actors and behaved in their roles with great confidence and assurance. Some have even pretended to be doctors, have deceived hospital authorities for a time, and have put patients in grave danger in order to fulfil their strange fantasy lives. Most of us enjoy playing a part sometimes.

In plays, dramas and theatrical productions we can learn our lines, put on costumes and make-up and seem – at a distance – to be someone else. We can look and sound like Macbeth or Hamlet, or Mark Antony, while the play lasts. But when the performance is over we take off our costumes, clean off the make-up, speak our own lines instead of Shakespeare's, and become ourselves again. School drama productions, and classroom play readings, are enjoyable and educationally valuable, but we should always take care never to carry our acting over into our real lives. It is very important indeed to be genuine, to be sincere, and to be ourselves. God wants us to be truly His, but also wants us to be truly ourselves. Polonius, a character in Shakespeare's "Hamlet", once said to his son, Laertes:-

"To thine own self be true,
And it must follow as the night the day,
Thou canst not then be false to any man."

Being true to God and true to ourselves is incalculably greater than being a clever actor and deceiving the people around us.

Prayer:

O God our Father, in Whom is perfect truth and total sincerity, help us always to be true to You and true to ourselves. Lord, You have given us our personalities and our characters. Make every one of us the best person that we can be, not trying to be what we are not, never pretending to be more than we are, never boasting, never deceiving others, and never deceiving ourselves. We ask it in the Name of our Lord Jesus Christ, whose perfect life and character are our pattern and guide for truth and consistency. Amen.

CHAPTER 32

The Family
God in our Homes

Scripture Reading: John 19:19-27

Key verse: John 19 verse 27: And from that hour that disciple took her unto his own home.

Hymn: Thou didst leave Thy throne, (Emily Elizabeth Steel Elliott 1836–1897).

As we have just heard in today's Scripture reading, even as He suffered the terrible agonies of crucifixion, Christ's thoughts were not for Himself but for others. It was very important to Him that Mary, His mother, should be well cared for, and so, in accordance with Hebrew custom at the time, He used a form of words which were rather like an adoption ceremony. John, the Beloved Disciple was to regard Mary as his own mother, and care for her accordingly. Mary was to regard John as her own son. There is one special word in our Key Verse, verse 27, that I want us to concentrate on this morning. That word is **home**. John, the Beloved Disciple of Jesus, took Mary into his own home. He was obeying his Lord's command, obeying it willingly and gladly. He now regarded Mary as a greatly loved, honoured, respected and permanent member of his own family so it was natural and right that he should take her home.

What is a home? What makes it so special and important to the people who live in it together? The ideal home is filled with love. It is a place where people care deeply for people, where husbands and wives love one another and parents love their children and grandchildren. It is a place where three or four generations of family can dwell in fellowship and mutual support, where the very oldest and the very youngest can feel wanted, needed, secure and loved. The oldest great-grand-parent and the tiniest great-grand-child are equally important members of the family in an ideal home.

The material wealth of a home is not of the least importance – it is only the wealth of love there that counts. Furniture may be worn and shabby, carpets threadbare, and curtains thin and frayed. There may not often be enough food and fuel. There may be no telephone, no fridge, no washing-machine, no television, no car and no record player. But if the people who live together in that home truly love one another, and care for one another, then there will be more happiness there than in a King's palace, a nobleman's castle, or a millionaire's mansion.

The people who share a loving home together need not necessarily be members of the same human family: Mary and John were not related. They were bound together by their common love and admiration of Jesus. A lodger or visitor can come to stay in a happy Christian home and feel himself to be part of the family because of the warmth of the welcome he receives there.

But we know, sadly, that many homes today are far from ideal. Parents quarrel with children and with each other. Children, striving to assert what they think of as their "rights" or their "independence" quarrel with parents and leave home. Grandparents and great-grandparents are thought of as a "nuisance" because they are old and need a little extra care and attention. They are sent into old people's homes "out of the way". Energetic youngsters are regarded as noisy and unwelcome and are encouraged to go out to give the adults "a bit of peace and quiet".

How sad and how wrong all this is! How far it is from the Christian ideal of real home and family life.

What is the answer? Every home can be good or bad, happy or unhappy, depending upon who is the head of the household. No home can be at its best unless Jesus Christ is the Head of the Household. If everyone in the family, every lodger and every visitor acknowledges Jesus as the Unseen Guest at every meal, the Unseen Witness to every action, and the Unseen Listener to every conversation, then that home will be a place of deep peace and great joy for all who share it.

Prayer:

Great Father of the whole human family, we praise and thank You for the joys of life in a loving Christian home. Grant us such awareness of the needs of other members of our own family that we may do all we can to support and strengthen them. Help us to contribute everything we can to our family's happiness and stability. Teach us so to love all the other members of our family, that we may always enjoy their fellowship and never regard them as difficult or unwelcome. Give us patience, kindness, good humour and tolerance, so that we may serve You by serving others, and help us to see that under Your Fatherhood all mankind are one great family in Christ. For His Name's sake, Amen.

CHAPTER 33

Trade and Commerce
God in the Shops

Scripture Reading: Amos 8:1-6
Key verse: Amos 8 verse 5: Making the ephah small and the shekel great.
Hymn: Fill Thou my life, O Lord my God, (Horatius Bonar, 1808–1889).

One of the jobs of a Weights and Measures Inspector today is to ensure that shops are providing their customers with the correct weight of flour, sugar, tea or whatever it is the customer is buying. Petrol pumps at service stations must be carefully and accurately calibrated and checked to ensure that they are actually delivering a full litre of petrol when they register a litre on their gauges. Sacks of coal usually contain either an old hundredweight or fifty modern kilogrammes. If a shopkeeper is unscrupulous, or dishonest, he can reduce the weight or measure of what he is selling, but still charge the customer the full price. At the time when the prophet Amos – the great advocate of social justice – was speaking to the Israelites, the **ephah** was a measure of capacity – like our litre, or gallon. The **shekel** was a coin. So when Amos accuses his hearers of "making the **ephah** small and the **shekel** great" he is saying that they are selling dishonestly small amounts at dishonestly high prices.

At the beginning of our reading Amos records how the Lord had shown him a vision of a basket of summer fruit. Then the prophet goes on to say that the end is coming for Israel. The point of Amos's statement is that the Hebrew word for "basket of fruit" (**qaits**) sounds very similar to the Hebrew word for "end" or "finish" (**qets**). We normally use similar sounding words as puns, but the Hebrews used them to emphasize important messages rather than to make jokes. It wasn't only the short measures and the high prices that Amos was criticizing. He was concerned with the **quality** of the goods as well. He accused the dishonest traders of selling "the refuse of the wheat".

When we go shopping today, we expect to be able to buy goods of satisfactory quality at a price we can afford, and we expect to receive the weight or quantity we've paid for. If we have been given short weight or if we've been overcharged for our goods, we expect the problem to be put right by the shop manager. As a last resort we – or a Weights and Measures Inspector – can see that justice is done in court.

But what would happen if the law courts themselves were corrupt? What would happen if wealthy shopkeepers and merchants could bribe judges and juries, and poor men could get no help from the courts? That was what things were like in the Northern Kingdom of Israel when Amos was proclaiming the need for justice and honesty. In those days a man who could not pay his debts – and that was difficult when prices were unfairly high – could be sold as a slave in order to settle the account. Amos spoke out fearlessly against this evil. He told the Israelites that they were selling men into slavery for debts as trifling as the price of a pair of shoes. He made it very clear to them that their elaborate religious ceremonies, sacrifices and services were of no interest to God unless the people were just, honest and fair in their trading.

Nowadays it is more likely that Amos would condemn the growing number of thieves who steal from shops than that he would criticize the shopkeepers. The curious modern word "shop-lifting" seems almost to excuse, or make light of, the sin of stealing. But from whichever side the dishonesty came, Amos would have spoken out boldly and fearlessly against it. When we ourselves are trading, buying or selling, there are a number of questions we should ask. Is this item I am selling in good condition? Is it working well? Will it give good service to the person who buys it? Knowing as much about it as I do, would I myself be happy to buy it for this price? Would I try to sell it at this price to my father, my elder brother, my employer, or the instructor at my Judo Club? Would I try to sell it at this price to someone I genuinely love, like, or respect? As Christians we should always ask ourselves whether we would be happy to carry out the transaction with the Lord watching and listening, because He is always with us, and always aware of everything we do. How often do we please Him? How often do we grieve Him?

Prayer:

O Lord of all Justice, Honesty and Integrity, You see and hear and know everything that we do. Help us to remember the words of Amos, Your prophet, who exhorted men to trade honestly with one another. Help us to be fair in all our dealings, to give good quality and generous measure, and to charge only honest and reasonable prices. Show us that true and acceptable worship consists far more of honesty in our dealings with others than with observing ritual and ceremony, and so help us to worship truly and acceptably. We ask it in the Name of Jesus Christ our Lord, Amen.

CHAPTER 34

Physics
God in matter and energy

Scripture Reading: Mark 4:35-41

Key verse: Mark 4 verse 41: What manner of man is this, that even the wind and the sea obey Him?

Hymn: Fierce raged the tempest o'er the deep, (Godfrey Thring, 1823–1903).

Physics has been described as that science which deals with the properties and interactions of matter and energy. Our modern word **physics** comes for a Greek word meaning **natural things,** and one of the attractions of physics is that it is a difficult science to limit, or define. Almost everything in our universe – including ourselves – involves matter and energy. "A mass of fifty kilogrammes moving at one metre per second . . ." could be a physicist's description of an average student entering the assembly hall this morning. The cook who is actually responsible for boiling the potatoes, or frying the chips, for today's lunch concentrates on getting the correct quantity of food ready at the correct time. A physicist observing that cooking process would be interested in the original mass of the potatoes, their initial temperature, the change of energy from gas or electricity into heat, and the way that heat was conducted into the potatoes. He would observe and measure, and then explain – in scientific terms – precisely what interactions had taken place between the matter which comprised the potatoes and the energy which had heated them. As a physicist rather than a chemist, a biologist or a dietician, he would not be as interested in the chemical changes which had taken place in the potato as a result of its exposure to heat. Something as familiar as walking into this hall, or cooking the lunch, is, in fact, a far more complex and involved process than it seems. The mysteries inside the atom, and the mysteries of the farthest galaxies are just as much a part of physics as the study of a student moving into this hall, or a cook preparing potatoes. Consider the famous Einstein equation

$$E = mc^2.$$

Matter and energy are interchangeable; in a sense, one is only a different **form** of the other. **One can turn into the other** in certain circumstances. The matter which makes up the physical bodies of cooks, or students, or potatoes has the same fundamental nature as the energy which boils water or takes us from the assembly hall to the library. We can control that fraction of those universal laws and forces which enable us to walk about, to cook our food, and do thousands of other everyday things.

Our God and Father created and controls those tremendous forces, and His Son, our Lord Jesus Christ, also has mastery over them. A physicist can measure and explain the scientific nature of a storm, the forces of winds and waves. Jesus subdued them.

When the nature of the smallest fundamental particle has been precisely described, and when the farthest galaxy has been fully explored, when physics can give us all the scientific answers about matter and energy, the Love of God, the saving power of Christ, and the eternal spiritual values He teaches will still remain supreme.

Prayer:

Almighty God, Lord of all energy, creator and upholder of all matter, help us to approach and explore the mysteries of Your universe with reverence and awe, that we may find You through what You have made for us. May we never forget Your eternal values of Love, joy and fellowship, which are infinitely more important than anything in this everyday world. Help us to reach and to hold on to those everlasting values, through Christ our Saviour, who went to the Cross in order that we might possess those good and eternal things. Amen.

CHAPTER 35

Words and Structures
God in Grammar

Scripture Reading: II Kings 22:8-13

Key verse: II Kings 22 verse 8: I have found the book of the law in the house of the Lord.

Hymn: Father of mercies in Thy word, (Anne Steele, 1716–1778).

The study of formal grammar and the technical structure of language are not often found in English lessons today. No doubt some of the most rigid of the old enthusiasts for formal grammar did make it into something dull, difficult and divorced from the art of saying what you mean in a clear and unmistakable way. But good grammar, well taught and thoroughly understood, will greatly increase our powers of expression in the language. Grammar is to language what law is to society. Grammar is to language what backbone is to a vertebrate animal. Grammar is to language what pit props are to a coal mine. Language without grammar would merely be words in chaos.

For example, English Grammar tells us what words do, what the function and purpose of a word is in its context. Nouns we know are the names, or labels, of things : a book, a piano, a hall, a school, a town – all nouns. It is the function of a noun to identify something by its name. The flat, round, metal object, which we exchange for goods and services is, of course, a coin. The word **coin** is a noun when we use it in this way. Some words can be used in very different ways although their spelling and pronunciation is the same in each case. A **seal** can be a piece of wax fixed to the end of a document. That is a noun. It gives a name to the piece of wax. A **seal** can also be a marine animal. He, too, is a noun. We **seal** envelopes or food containers. Here **seal** is no longer a noun but a verb, a word which denotes action. If we expand the idea by talking of a **strong** seal, a **hermetic** seal, or a **broken** seal, we are using adjectives – **strong, hermetic** and **broken** – to "describe" or qualify nouns. An adjective tells us something more about a noun. **Large, small, blue, green, old** and **young** are all adjectives. Grammar keeps these different parts of speech in their rightful places, and provides us with a system for combining them effectively into phrases, clauses and sentences with clear meanings.

When the book of the Law was found during repairs to the Temple, as we read in today's portion of Scripture, the King, the priests and the prophetess took its message very seriously. They knew that the sacred rules had not been kept properly, and they were very concerned to put things right. If someone has been speaking and writing incorrectly for years and then finds a good grammar book which shows him his mistakes, he may decide – as King Josiah decided – to try his best to improve by following the instructions in the book.

It is quite important to rid our speech and writing of such clumsy and ungrammatical things as double negatives, subjects which don't agree with their verbs, and split infinitives. It is incomparably more important – eternally important – to rid our lives of sin and selfishness by reading and trying to obey the Divine Grammar of Morality, the Book of God's Law, as Josiah did of old. But we must remember that our human strength and human will is not enough to achieve anything. We need strength from outside ourselves. By the Grace of God, we have not only the Law which King Josiah had, but we have the saving power of Christ which enables us to keep that Law.

Prayer:

O God, our heavenly Father, Author and Giver of all Scripture and all Truth, the Maker of Divine Law, help us to respond to Your rules and words of guidance, as King Josiah and his people responded of old. Help us to realise that only with the help of Your Son, our Lord Jesus Christ, can we keep and honour Your Sacred Law, and only through His Purity can we become pure. We ask these prayers in the precious Name of that same Jesus Christ, who perfected the Law and fulfilled the Prophets, Amen.

CHAPTER 36

Wood and Craftsmanship
God in Carpentry

Scripture Reading: Matthew 11:28-30 and Matthew 13:53-57

Key verse: Matthew 13 verse 55: Is not this the carpenter's son?

Hymn: Lord of all hopefulness, Lord of all joy, (Jan Struthers, 1901–1953).

There is a special privilege about working with wood, from the simplest piece of D.I.Y. shelf-fixing to the creation of a beautiful and elaborate piece of furniture like a hand-carved eighteenth century desk. Jesus himself worked with wood at the carpenter's shop in Nazareth. Of all the trades, jobs, professions and vocations, it was carpentry that was honoured and sanctified by Jesus Himself.

In the beginning of all things, He created all things with His Father. Jesus was and is that Living Word of God, that Word of Power who spoke and it was done, who called the galactic universe into being. This infinitely powerful Son of God came to earth in the form of Man, was born in a stable at Bethlehem, grew up and worked as a carpenter in Nazareth.

When a skilled carpenter touches a piece of wood he can make it into something strong and useful. When Jesus, the Supreme Carpenter, touches a person, He makes that person into someone strong, useful and good. There are many different ways in which a carpenter can shape wood. He can saw it, plane it, drill it, smooth it and carve it. When we turn to Jesus and ask Him to share our lives He can cut away those sins and weaknesses which we want to be rid of. He can plane off the rough edges, the sharp words, the vicious temper, our timidity, deceit and cowardice, and reveal the true grain and colour of all that we really long to be. He can drill holes through our selfishness, pride and isolation, so that we can be fixed firmly to Him and to other Christians in everlasting fellowship. He can smooth away every hurt, calming our distress, comforting our sorrows and taking away our fear. He can carve His sign on our hearts – the emblem of victory, the token of everlasting light and joy, the assurance that every debt is paid and every sin forgiven: the Cross of Calvary.

As a carpenter in Nazareth in first century Palestine, Jesus would have made yokes for oxen to pull against, and for people to wear across their shoulders to carry heavy weights. We can picture in our minds the care and concern Jesus would have had as an expert carpenter, and as a craftsman with proper pride in His work, as He made sure His yokes fitted well, and were as smooth as possible.

The Gospel is not only a challenge to stand boldly and fight for Christ, to use all our strength and energy in God's service, it is also an assurance of rest, peace, tranquillity and joy. The Great Carpenter has said: **My yoke is easy and my burden is light.**

Prayer:

O loving heavenly Father, we thank You for the gift of our Lord Jesus Christ who came from the glory of heaven to work as a Carpenter in Nazareth for our sakes, and for our salvation. Help us to think of Him each time we work with wood, and each time that we admire the craftsmanship and skill of others who work with wood. May we always try to work as conscientiously as He worked, and to care as He did for those for whom the work is being done. We ask these prayers in the Name of Him who worked with wood as well as with men, and who always brought out the best from whatever He worked with, Jesus Christ, Galilean Carpenter and Lord of all, Amen.

CHAPTER 37

Reference and Precedent
God in the Library

Scripture Reading: Luke 24:25-35

Key verse: Luke 24 verse 32: Did not our heart burn within us, while He talked with us by the way, and while He opened to us the scriptures?

Hymn: The Spirit breathes upon the word, (William Cowper, 1731–1800).

Melvil Dewey was a American Librarian who gave his name to the Dewey Decimal System of classifying and cataloguing library books. Born in 1851, Dewey put forward his ideas in 1876 while he was working at Amherst College in Massachusetts. In 1877 he was a co-founder and editor of the **Library Journal.**

In the Dewey Decimal system books are given numerical classifications which range from 000, which means **General**, up to 900, which is **History.** By using additional numbers, the classifications can be subdivided again. For example, **Literature** in general is 800, **American Literature** is 810, and **English Literature** is 820.

One of the most important functions of an educational library is to provide reference books for research purposes. Those books need to be carefully classified and arranged for quick and convenient access by the students and research workers who need the information. To make progress with a piece of research, we not only need to have as much information as we can obtain, we must have it in a well organised and accessible form. It has to be easy to retrieve whenever we want it.

As an example of the different directions in which research can lead, a few years ago the author and his wife were researching a book on the mystery of the priest's treasure at Rennes-le-Château in south-western France. Exactly what that treasure was and how the priest, Bérenger Saunière, came to find it are still wide open for discussion. However, the research the author and his wife did while compiling their book included Roman coinage and Roman gold mines, the Visigoths, Dagobert II, Louis XIV, Nicholas Poussin (the seventeenth century painter), the Habsburg Dynasty and a monument in the grounds of Shugborough Hall in Staffordshire.

Curiously enough, all of those topics – and some even stranger ones – had a contribution to make to the mystery. Good reference libraries, where information is accurately classified and readily available, make it possible to find out what researchers need to know.

The best of all libraries is to be found in the sixty-six books of the Holy Bible: thirty-nine in the Old Testament and twenty-seven in the New Testament. Each book is divided into chapters and verses so that particular passages of Scripture can be referred to accurately and found easily. One of the most helpful books for Bible readers, students, preachers and ministers to refer to is **Cruden's Concordance.** This gives a list of all the words in the Bible in alphabetical order, then indicates the book, chapter and verse where each may be found. Suppose, for example, that you were looking for a text about studying. The **Concordance** gives us the reference Proverbs 15:28 where we find, **"The heart of the righteous studieth to answer : but the mouth of the wicked poureth out evil things."** Alexander Cruden, was born in 1701 and died in 1770. He did for Bible readers what Melvil Dewey did for the Library Service, and we owe a debt of gratitude to them both. There is no research as important as studying the Scriptures, for in them we find the Living Word, our Lord Jesus Christ, whom to know is life eternal.

Prayer:

O loving Lord, the Fount of all wisdom and all knowledge, You have provided the Holy Scriptures for our guidance and learning. Help us to understand Your Word. Open its truth to us, as the Risen Lord opened its truth to those two disciples on the road to Emmaus long ago. May we never tire of reading and re-reading its message of life, of light and of salvation, and may we share with many others, the everlasting treasure we find in its pages. We ask these prayers in the name of Him who understood and explained the Scriptures perfectly to His disciples, Jesus Christ our Saviour, Amen.

CHAPTER 38

Streets and Meadows
God in the City and God in the Countryside

Scripture Reading: Luke 15:11-24

Key verse: Luke 15 verse 18: I will arise and go to my father.

Hymn: There were ninety and nine that safely lay, (Elizabeth Cecilia Clephane, 1830–1869).

Jesus told several parables about the lost and the found : a woman lost a silver coin, a shepherd lost one of his sheep, a man lost his son. Most teachers have had the experience of an anxious parent telephoning the school in the late afternoon because a son or daughter has not arrived home at the expected time. It is a very great relief and joy to parents and staff alike when that lost pupil turns up safely having gone to a friend's home for tea without thinking to let the family know first!

The parable which formed our Scripture reading today is often called **The Parable of the Prodigal Son.** That word **prodigal** means recklessly wasteful, or lavish. A prodigal spends money carelessly and without making any provision for future needs. It is a story which shows how thoroughly Jesus understood human nature, and how similar people are despite the passage of centuries. In the film "**Star Wars**" young Luke, the hero, is very tired of working and living in his uncle's remote country home. He wants adventure. He craves for what he thinks is the excitement of city life. "**Star Wars**" is fiction, but the young man's longing for excitement and adventure in the big city is a true and accurate reflection of the way that many young people think. Like the prodigal son in Jesus's parable, many of them find only hardship, misery and disillusionment. The fortunate ones realise in time that home is best, and go back as the prodigal son in the parable went back. It is greatly to be hoped that their parents will react just as the father did in Christ's parable.

Of course, there are advantages and disadvantages in city life and in country life. Each has its good and bad points. There are flourishing city churches, and lively city Christian fellowships which reach out to help the people around them. There is also crime and corruption, temptation, sin and depravity on a massive scale in many cities. Some small country communities can be spoilt by pettiness, jealousy and bitter feuding over ridiculous little issues that

94

have no importance at all. There may be nothing in the village for people to do, and nowhere for them to go.

The country village, the busy town, the teeming city: each can provide us with an ideal home if we put God at the forefront of our personal lives, and at the head of our community.

Prayer:

O Lord our God, Ruler of land and sea, town and country, city and village, help us to seek and acknowledge You wherever we live and wherever we go. Show us what is good and beautiful in the quiet peace of the countryside. Reveal to us Your Energy and Purpose in the noise and activity of great cities. Help us to find You in the streets and market places of busy towns. We ask it in the Name of our Lord Jesus Christ, who was born in the town of Bethlehem, preached in the countryside of Galilee, and died for us in the city of Jerusalem, Amen.

CHAPTER 39

Computers and Keyboards
God in Technology

Scripture Reading: Ecclesiastes 9:11-18

Key verse: Ecclesiastes 9 verse 15: He by his wisdom delivered the city.

Hymn: From Thee all skill and science flow, (Charles Kingsley 1819–1875).

Some thinkers would define **technology** as the process by which ideas are turned into physical realities. Thomas Alva Edison, the American inventor, was born in 1847 and lived until 1931. During his long and productive life he patented more than 1,000 inventions. He worked on them continually at his combined workshop and laboratory at Menlo Park, and then at West Orange, for over fifty years. He took out his first patent in 1868. This was an electrical vote recording machine for use in elections. He patented his "phonograph or speaking machine" in 1877. On October 21st, 1879 after spending over $40,000 – an enormous sum of money in those days – on experiments and tests that all failed, Edison finally succeeded in making an electric light bulb with a carbonized cotton filament, or thread, glowing in a vacuum. This filament was incandescent: it gave out more light than heat, and it lasted for over forty hours. The original **idea** was to pass an electric current through **something** to make it glow and give out light. Finding out what that **something** ought to be, and how to make it work reliably for a long time, was what cost $40,000 and thousands of hours of experimental work. Making the idea into a light bulb that actually worked was technology.

In the **"Arabian Nights"** stories there were flying carpets. Men had dreamed of flying for centuries before **technology** first took a balloon into the air in 1783, and the Wright brothers struggled to get their primitive wood and canvas aeroplane a few feet off the ground for the first powered flight in December of 1903.

Many accountants and bankers must have dreamed of a machine which would do their calculations for them at the touch of a button, long before calculators and computers were invented. Electronic technology and the silicon chip made those dreams come true.

But technology does not progress in a simple line, like arithmetical numbers. We do not have one invention, two inventions, three inventions and so on. Technology progresses exponentially or geometrically: that is it tends to double its size at each step, instead of moving in a simple line. Technology advances at the rate of one, two, four, eight, sixteen . . . not at the rate of one, two, three, four . . . Computers help to build bigger and more powerful computers. The next generation of computers will be more like **thinking** machines than **adding** machines!

A technician at a keyboard in the twentieth century has a great deal more responsibility than a scribe with a parchment scroll in the first century Yet one thing – the only thing that matters – does not change. Both men have a choice to make between good and evil. The technician at the computer keyboard can solve a problem in medicine or work out some cunning method of robbing a credit card company by "hacking" into their security programme. The scribe can write that God is love, or a letter to the High Priest plotting against Jesus. God does not judge us by the power of our technology but by the moral decisions we make about how to **use our technology.**

Prayer:

Almighty God, from whom all wisdom and knowledge come, help us to use the wisdom You have given us in the right way. Help us to devise technologies of healing and learning, of good and fair industry and commerce, of clear and loving communications. Help us to think more of our duties and responsibilities to others and less of our own rights and privileges. Grant us the grace to know that wherever technology may lead us in the future, it can never lead us beyond the reach of your fatherly care. Help us to remember that nothing can separate us from the love of Christ, in Whose Name we ask these prayers. Amen.

CHAPTER 40

Health Education, Safety and First Aid
God in Caring and Protecting

Scripture Reading: Psalm 27:1-14

Key verse: Psalm 27 verse 14: Wait on the Lord: be of good courage, and He shall strengthen thine heart.

Hymn: I sing the almighty power of God, (Isaac Watts, 1674–1748).

The psalmist lived in a dangerous world – a world of warfare and enemies, a world where a traveller could be attacked by wild beasts, or thieves, a world where diseases and accidents were well known. He turned to the Lord for protection and security because he knew that God loved him and cared for him.

We also live in a dangerous world, and the psalmist's decision to put his trust in God is the best decision for us too.

When a tightrope walker is keeping her balance on the swaying wire, she has to be very careful to maintain a central position. Going too far to the left or to the right will cause her to fall. In a dangerous world, we need the skills of tightrope walkers. Going too far towards the side of safety, caution and protectiveness means that we shall experience no adventures at all. We may manage to observe a little of life second-hand, as it goes past, but we shall not **live** it. Going too far towards rashness, recklessness and mindless disregard for safety can bring us, and those who try to rescue us, into terrible and unnecessary danger. There are times, of course, when our service to God and to our brothers and sisters demands that we should have as little regard for our own safety as Christ had for His when He went to the cross for us. There are other times when it is right to think hard about health and safety. There were times when Elijah the prophet stood up publicly and fearlessly against King Ahab, Queen Jezebel and the priests of Baal. There were also times when he hid. John the Baptist died for his fearless and outspoken criticism of King Herod and Queen Herodias. Moses challenged Pharaoh face to face with God's strength to support him, but the same Moses had once fled from Egypt in fear of his life after killing the Egyptian task-master who was ill-treating a Hebrew slave.

When Jesus was tempted by Satan at the beginning of His public ministry, He refused to put God's protective providence to the test by making a spectacular jump from the highest point of the Temple, but He did not hesitate to use His power to still the storm, **when it was necessary.** God never wants us to take unnecessary risks, or to act rashly or recklessly. Only a very stupid person explores a pothole when heavy rain is expected, and his stupidity endangers those who volunteer for the rescue party. God does, however, expect us to do His will regardless of the cost. Only a weakling and a fool deliberately sets out to ruin his health with addictive drugs, cigarettes, alcohol and promiscuity. A Christian hero or heroine goes through jungles and swamps, across deserts and mountains, into leper colonies and tropical fever hospitals, **when called by Christ to carry His Gospel to those places.**

In school we can learn about healthy living, sensible diet, first aid and safety. We learn why it is sensible not to smoke, why we should cut down on our intake of fat, salt and sugar, and what to do to help a patient with a broken arm, or a deep cut which is bleeding rapidly. In life we can learn to minimise the dangers we face, while at the same time going where God wants us to go. The missionary working among cholera victims is first innoculated against cholera. The Gospel messenger carrying a canoe load of Bibles along a dangerous river wears a life jacket, and picks the safest route through the rapids. Two old proverbs sum up the message well, and both relate to the old-time navy. The first is: "Trust in God, but row away from the rocks." The second dates from the days of muzzle loading cannons that used gunpowder: "Trust in God, and keep your powder dry." We might make up a new one for ourselves: "When God sends you to rescue an injured climber on the mountain, take ropes and the proper equipment when you go."

Prayer:

Loving heavenly Father, You have given us courage and a spirit of adventure. Never let us lead others into danger because of our recklessness. You have given us thoughtful minds and taught us to be prudent and careful. Never let us hang back through fear when You call us to go forward to help others. Help us to learn from the example of our Lord Jesus Christ when to speak and act boldly and when to wait quietly for Your guidance. Let us never confuse rashness with courage, or cowardice with caution, but grant us the wisdom to know Your Will and the strength to carry it out, for the sake of Him who always carried out Your Will to perfection, Jesus Christ our Lord, Amen.

CHAPTER 41

**Philosophy and Logic
God in our Thinking**

Scripture Reading: Acts 17:16-28
Key verse: Acts 17 verse 28: For in Him we live, and move, and have our being.
Hymn: My God, how wonderful Thou art, (Frederick William Faber, 1814–1863).

The dictionary defines **Philosophy** as seeking after wisdom or knowledge, and seeking especially for that knowledge which is concerned with ultimate reality, the **true** nature of things, fundamental causes and principles. Philosophy is interested in the **Why? What? When? Where?** and **How?** of Life. Philosophy is concerned with answering the deepest riddles of the universe. It is said that a famous university set an entrance examination for its philosophy students on which the first question was the single word "**Why?**" A student who would be likely to do well on a philosophy course at university would be able to write several pages in answer to that.

Plato once said that the unexamined life was not worth living. If we don't pause to **think** about what we are, why we're here, and where we're going, we might just as well be cabbages in a garden or diesel engines on a railway. Let us spend one or two minutes this morning examining our lives. Start with ourselves, think of our own individual identities, ask ourselves who we are and what kind of characters we have. Are we good, bad or indifferent people? Go outwards from ourselves to our families and friends. How do we fit into our family group and how do our friends see us? Go further out still into the whole school community. Ask yourself what your role is in the school, and what part you play in the life of the school. Go wider still into our county, our country, our continent and our world. What is your place as a citizen? How do you measure up against all the rest of the human race? Finally, go right out into the galactic universe where our huge earth itself seems only like a tiny speck of dust between great stars separated by unimaginable distances. That's just one brief way of looking at ourselves, and trying to examine our lives. There are many, many other examinations to be made as we search for philosophical understanding.

As we read in the Scriptures, Paul, the great missionary and evangelist of the first century, once visited Athens. The Athenians loved philosophy. They delighted in hearing new ideas and then arguing about them. Athens was a great market place for philosophical ideas, and Paul used that as a basis for his sermon.

The trouble with many of the Athenians who heard Paul was that they had forgotten – if they had ever known in the first place – what true philosophy was about. Some people are so fond of arguing for its own sake, they get so much pleasure merely from fighting with words, they forget that the only sensible reason for arguing is to try to establish or discover truth.

Paul wanted to teach them the soul-saving truth about the love of God the Father and the redeeming work of God the Son on Calvary. Sadly many of the Athenians listening to Paul were more interested in the battle of ideas than with the truth about salvation.

The dictionary defines **Logic** as the science of reasoning, proof or inference. There is **inductive** logic in which general laws, or facts, are inferred from a number of instances. For example, if five or six of your friends all said they had enjoyed a very good holiday at a certain campsite near Skegness, you could reason by inductive logic that it was a good campsite, and you might well decide to go there yourself next year.

Deductive logic works the other way round. It starts out from general laws, or principles, and argues from them to particular cases. If you start with the general principal or "law" that all cats chase mice, you discover mice in your garage so you put a cat in to chase them. However, deductive logic **may** let you down occasionally! Your particular cat may not be interested in mice at all or may want to make friends with them!

God wants us to think. He has given us minds and reasoning power and a healthy curiosity about the universe He has made for us. But our curiosity is not an end in itself. It is a spur to look for what really matters. We must be better philosophers than the Athenians to whom Paul spoke. We must not look at ideas merely for the sake of looking. We must always look for truth. We must also be careful how we use our reasoning powers. We must use our reasoning powers to examine our reasoning powers. We must use our logic to test our logic.

Professor C. S. Lewis, undoubtedly one of the great geniuses of our century, and a man of superb reasoning power, was brought to Christ through that very reasoning power which God had given him. Faith in Christ and clear, honest reasoning are good companions. They can live happily and harmoniously together in the same human mind. God gave us our power to think. Let us use it for Him as C. S. Lewis did.

Prayer:
All wise and loving Father, You gave us minds that can think, and question, and reason. Help us so to use our reasoning powers that our philosophy and our logic may ever lead us to the truth about You and Your Son, Jesus Christ our Lord, in whose Name we ask these prayers. Amen.

CHAPTER 42

Close of Year or Close of Term
God in our Endings

Scripture Reading: Psalm 72:11-20

Key verse: Psalm 72 verse 20: The prayers of David the son of Jesse are ended.

Hymn: God be in my head, (Horae B. V. Mariae, 1514, Sarum Primer, 1558).

From the point of view of the sun there is no such thing as the ending of the day. As it sets over one land, it rises on another. As the twilight of evening falls in one place, so the twilight of early morning brightens in another. As the hymn writer reminds us in **The day Thou gavest, Lord is ended,** the same sun that bids us rest " . . . is waking our brethren 'neath the western skies." Beginnings and endings are only appearances. God's eternity is the only absolute reality.

We read in Psalm 72 today, how King David ended his prayers. Of course, they were not ended forever, only for the time being. One of the favourite questions in English vocabulary tests used to be to ask the student to distinguish between **continuously** and **continually.** The first means going on and on without stopping. The second means going on for a while, pausing for a time, and going on again, having recurring periods of activity with intervals between them. We would say, for example, that a cyclist in hilly country was **continually** dismounting to walk up the hills. The same cyclist on holiday in a flat country, like Holland, might well be able to pedal **continuously** – without any break at all – for three or four hours at a time.

David prayed **continually** throughout his life. He also fought **continually** against his country's enemies, principally the Philistines. He was a skilled musician, too. He played the harp **continually.** He wrote Psalms **continually.** An ending for David in that sense was, therefore, not a permanent or final ending. His wars, his music and his prayers were interrupted from time to time, but sooner or later they were resumed.

When we drop a subject we have been studying in school we have not really given it up forever. For example we may decide not to take history as an examination subject when we choose our options for the fourth year, but we shall undoubtedly read historical novels, watch historical films, enjoy historical biographies and argue over the causes of historical events from time to time throughout our future lives.

We should never think of endings as being as permanent as they seem to be. In the Conan Doyle story entitled **The Final Problem** we read about the supposed end of Sherlock Holmes in the Reichenbach Falls. We are led to believe that the great fictional detective plunged to his death locked in a hand to hand struggle with the arch-criminal, Professor Moriarty. However, much to the delight of millions of readers, Holmes turns up again, alive and well, and the mystery of his apparent death is explained in **The Adventure of the Empty House.** Only a story, of course, but one from which we can learn an important lesson: endings are not always as final as they look. During World War One, 1914–1918, the Revd. Studdert Kennedy was a padre, or army chaplain. In one of his great Christian poems about faith he wrote that death " . . . **was not anything but Satan's lie upon eternal life."**

Our eternal God goes on although everything else may seem to have ended. All good and worthwhile things are rooted and grounded in Him, and He will never allow any good thing to perish. Psalm 34 verse 10 tells us how they that serve the Lord shall not want for any good thing, and in Psalm 16 verse 11 we read that at God's right hand there are pleasures for evermore.

Prayer:

Eternal Lord, grant us the wisdom to understand that there is no ending to Your love and no limit to Your power. As the day, the week, the term or the year ends help us to see new beginnings, new horizons and new opportunities ahead of us. Help us to go forward confidently, secure in Your love, and trusting You in all things new and old. Be with us, Lord, in every ending and every beginning, for the sake of Jesus Christ our Lord, Amen.

CHAPTER 43

New Terms, New Years and New Pupils
God in our Beginnings

Scripture Reading: Revelation 21:1-7

Key verse: Revelation 21 verse 5: Behold, I make all things new.

Hymn: New every morning is the love, (J. Keble, 1792–1866).

A pessimist will look at a cup of water when he is thirsty and regard it as **half-empty.** An optimist looking at the water level in the same cup will say it is **half-full.** Sometimes people have to leave old friends, old homes where they have lived happily for many years, a previous school which they have enjoyed attending, a village, a town, a city or country, where they once lived contentedly. The pessimist thinks hard about what he is leaving behind, what he is giving up and what he is losing because of the change. An optimist balances those regrets by thinking of all that is good, all there is to look forward to, and all the opportunities for service in the new environment. We can look at changes in our lives in two ways – as endings or as beginnings.

As we read in the Scripture this morning, God makes all things new. We can think of the meaning of that Key Verse in a number of ways. God our Creator, Sustainer and Renewer, takes old things that have gone wrong and puts them right. He makes them as good as new. When a car radiator, an alternator, or a starter motor fails, it is sometimes sent back to a special factory or workshop to be reconditioned. There it is checked over thoroughly, rebuilt and restored until it is as good as new. God takes a human life that has failed and reconditions it like that: He makes it new again. But because He loves us so much and respects that freewill and individual personality which He has given each one of us, He will not recondition our lives until we ask Him. He will not come in until we invite Him in. God's kind of renewal and reconditioning is not a replacement. He does not make a repentant sinner into someone else. We very definitely remain ourselves after God has worked His miracle of salvation in our lives. We are not **less** of ourselves, but more, **far more.** With God's help we are at last becoming our real selves. We lose our **selfishness** and **self-centredness** but we gain instead something wonderful which we might try to describe as **selfness.** A starter motor that will not work is not truly a starter motor. If it had a mind and was aware of itself and its problems, it might long to work properly, to be a real starter motor. A three-hundred year old painting, a great masterpiece, may have lain lost, covered with dirt and grime in a cellar, for many of those years. At last it is found and taken to a skilled restorer. His loving work gradually reveals all the potential beauty of the picture, and eventually it hangs in the National Gallery – in its rightful place. No one would have thought that the blackened canvas square decaying in a corner of the cellar was a masterpiece. Our lives are often like that lost picture, until we put them into the nail-pierced hands of the Great Restorer who makes all things new.

Prayer:

Our loving heavenly Father, Maker and Restorer of all things, help us at this time to make a new start in our own lives. Help us to open our hearts and minds to You, to invite You to make us new men and women, walking always in Christ's Way and following the path of true discipleship. We ask these prayers in and through the Name of Him who restored mankind, regardless of the cost to Himself, Jesus Christ our Lord, Amen.

CHAPTER 44

Fields, Vineyards and Olives
God in our Harvest

Scripture Reading: Matthew 13:1-9, 18-23

Key verse: Matthew 13 verse 23: But he that received seed into the good ground is he that heareth the word and understandeth it; which also beareth fruit, and bringeth forth, some an hundredfold, some sixtyfold and some thirtyfold.

Hymn: We plough the fields and scatter, (Matthias Claudius, 1740–1815).
(Translated by Jane Montgomery Campbell 1817–1878)

In the Parable of the Sower, Jesus teaches us that although the Word of God is freely available to all, not everyone benefits from that opportunity. Some people are so resistant to it – as hard as well trodden paths – that the Word does not really penetrate their minds. It is snatched away from them by the forces of evil even before they take it in. Others are so busy with the things of this world – anxiety and ambition, poverty and wealth, fame and success, career and reputation, pleasure and politics, hobbies and pastimes – that they neglect the Word. Instead of concentrating on the spiritual things that really matter, these people allow the trivial and temporary things of this world to destroy the eternal things which are trying to grow in their hearts and minds. These people are like neglected farms and gardens where the weeds and brambles have taken over and destroyed the crops.

In this parable, Jesus warns us against being shallow characters. He teaches us that such people are like stony ground, where the soil is very thin. The seed springs up well at first, but as soon as the sun gets hot the plants wither and die because they have no proper roots and no moisture. We all know people like this; sometimes, when we examine our own characters carefully and honestly, we wonder if we ourselves are in this category – at least some of the time. Jesus says that such people start off to follow Him enthusiastically, but they give up when circumstances become difficult. There's a very good saying, which is well worth remembering: **When the going gets tough, the tough get going.** Christianity does for the character what weight-training and hard physical exercise do for the body – it toughens us. Shallow people who have no depth of character are weak, but Christ can give strength even to them, if they invite Him into their lives and ask for His help. That help enables them eventually to be like the fourth type of land: the good land.

There are people with clear, open, honest and receptive minds, who receive the Word gladly and act on it sincerely, who welcome Christ into everything they do and become His faithful workers to their lives' ends – which is only another name for the point at which Christ's eternal and abundant life takes over.

The parable that Jesus used was based on the harvest of the land, the harvest of corn. But there are many other types of harvest: the harvest of the sea, the harvest of industrial production, of mining, of oil drilling, of the mind – what might be termed the harvest of invention and discovery.

Whether we are harvesting corn, fish or technology, the principle remains the same. The harvest principle – the large return from the small sowing – is evidence of God's limitless generosity and abundant provision – if only we will learn to use His gifts properly, and share all our harvests with those in need.

Prayer:

Lord of all harvests, of the land and of the sea, of minds and of machines, help us to understand Your gifts and praise You best by using them aright for the benefit of others. As we celebrate the abundance of our own harvest teach us to share it with those in need, for the sake of Him who shared all He had with us, Jesus Christ our Lord, Amen.

CHAPTER 45

Christmas
God in the Manger

Scripture Reading: Luke 2:1-20

Key verse: Luke 2 verse 7: And she brought forth her first-born Son, and wrapped Him in swaddling clothes and laid Him in a manger; because there was no room for them in the inn.

Hymn: Hark! the herald-angels sing, (Charles Wesley, 1707–1788).

There is a huge contrast between the smallness and helplessness of a new born baby and the limitless power of the omnipotent and eternal God who called the universe into being. It is far greater than the contrast between the smallness of the hydrogen atom and the power of the hydrogen bomb. Compare one drop of rain with the great torrent which pours over Niagara Falls every second. Measure one grain of sand beside the vast expanse of the Sahara Desert. For all the differences between those dramatic contrasts, there is also an undeniable similarity, a quality that links the macrocosm to the microcosm – the greatest to the smallest. The tiny Babe is still very God of very God – and the Almighty God becomes the Babe for our sakes. The hydrogen atom and the hydrogen bomb are related by their physical and chemical properties. Water is the same basic substance whether it is falling gently, a drop at a time on a window box of flowers, or pouring over Niagara. Sand is still sand – a grain at a time, a ton at a time, or a desert at a time. You do not change the essential nature of a substance simply by changing its quantity.

The essential nature of God is Love. That doesn't change. God is Love whether He is creating and sustaining His entire universe, or sleeping in Mary's arms in the stable at Bethlehem.

What God shows us in Bethlehem is that there is nothing so small and helpless that He cannot enter it, and what He shows us in the physical universe is that there is nothing so large and powerful that He cannot control it. But God in the Babe or God in the galaxy is still the same loving God Whom Jesus taught us to call our Father.

Prayer:

Almighty and all loving Lord, we give thanks to You at this Christmas season for the stars you control in the infinite vastness of space, and for the one special star that led the Wise Men to Bethlehem. Help us to understand that You are in all things – the greatest and the least – and give us grace to invite the Christ Child into our hearts as we remember how there was no room for Him at the inn. We ask it for the sake of Him to whom the shepherds came, and for whom the holy angels sang, Jesus Christ, the Babe of Bethlehem, our Lord, our Redeemer and our God, Amen.

CHAPTER 46

Epiphany
The Revealing of God in Christ

Scripture Reading: Matthew 2:1-12

Key verse: Matthew 2 verse 11: They saw the young child with Mary His mother, and fell down and worshipped Him.

Hymn: As with gladness men of old, (William Chatterton Dix, 1837–1898).

The Christian celebration of Epiphany commemorates the arrival of the Magi, the Wise Men, the Eastern Kings, who came to see the new born Christ, to worship Him, to bring Him rare and costly gifts. Our word **Epiphany** comes from the Greek. The first part, the prefix **Epi-**, can mean **upon, above** or **in addition to.** The second part of the word conveys the idea of **showing, demonstrating,** or **revealing.** So we can think of the Epiphany of Jesus as the showing to mankind, represented by the three Magi, of Someone **higher** than man, Someone **above** man, Someone with qualities **in addition** to anything that man possessed.

The revealing of God to man is at its clearest, fullest and most perfect in Jesus. God reveals Himself to us through His Inspired Word, the Bible, through worship and Christian fellowship in our churches, through the warmth and love of Christian families and friends, and through the natural universe which He has created for us. He also reveals Himself to us through prayer and meditation, and in Christian art and music.

Jesus revealed God to the disciples by His miracles of healing, and His command over nature. He showed them more and more about God the Father in everything He did, and He revealed more and more about the loving nature of the Father in everything He said. He told parables – apparently simple stories with deep spiritual meanings – which revealed further truths about His Father and the coming of God's Kingdom.

The three symbolic gifts brought by the Magi at Epiphany were gold, frankincense and myrrh. Gold was an appropriate gift for a King; myrrh – the resin from the trees known as **Commiphora** – is used in perfumes and medicines, but was also used as a burial ointment. The gift of myrrh showed that one day this King would die to save His people. Frankincense is an aromatic resin from trees known as **Boswellia.** The word **frankincense** once meant the very best kind of incense, the highest quality. Only the very best was good enough to offer to Jesus. The gift of frankincense indicated that Jesus was not only King – He was God.

Prayer:

O Loving Heavenly Father, open our spiritual eyes at this season of Epiphany and reveal to us the truth about Your Son, our Lord Jesus Christ. Help us to understand as those wise Men from the East understood, that this same Jesus who was born in a stable and died for us on a cross, is both our Everlasting King and our Almighty God. We ask it in His Holy Name, Amen.

CHAPTER 47

The Season of Lent
God in Preparation

Scripture Reading: II Kings 3:9-20

Key verse: II Kings 3 verse 16: Thus saith the Lord, Make this valley full of ditches.

Hymn: Praise to the Lord, the Almighty, the King of Creation, (Joachim Neander, 1650–1680).
(Translated by Catherine Winkworth, 1829–1878, and others).

In today's Scripture reading we heard how three kings went out together to fight against the Moabites. In those days and in that area armies depended on their supplies of food and water – particularly **water.** Seven days journey into hostile territory, and the armies of the three Kings were desperate for fresh water supplies. Victory or defeat depended upon it.

They consulted Elisha the prophet, and he told them what to do : **make preparations, get ready.** In the case of these Kings, the exact form of their preparation was to dig ditches across the valley ready to hold the water which Elisha said would come. And there was more. The prophet told them that not only would the Lord send them the water which was vital for their survival, but He would also give them complete and overwhelming victory in the coming battle. Everything happened as Elisha had prophesied : the water came, and the Moabites were heavily defeated. The three Kings had obeyed the prophet and made the necessary preparations. Great success had followed.

The church's season of Lent is a time of preparation for the great celebration of Easter. During Lent Christian people begin to get ready to remember how Christ defeated the forces of evil at Calvary. That was an infinitely greater victory than the victory of the three Kings over the Moabites.

All through Scripture we can find similar examples of men and women of faith who prepared for a blessing which God had promised – and the blessing always came. Abraham left his home in faith – and God made him the founder of a great nation. Elijah prepared his sacrifice on Mount Carmel, and God blessed him by defeating the priests of Baal. Our Lord Jesus Christ went to the

Cross in faith and perfect obedience to His Father's Will. There He won His Unique Victory over sin and death, followed by the glorious blessing of the Resurrection. His anguished prayer and lonely vigil in the Garden of Gethsemane were part of His preparation for His world shaking conflict and ultimate victory over evil.

Preparation is a vital part of success. There was a school in Norfolk where the author began teaching back in the 1950s which had as its school motto : **Nihil sine labore** which is Latin for **Nothing without work.** It is an old proverb, but still a true one. The work of preparation is essential for success. If we keep a good Lent by thinking every day of the true meaning of Easter, we shall benefit so much more from the celebration of Easter when it comes. Is there something we can give up for Lent to help others, and to remind us in a practical way that Christ our Lord gave up everything for us? Shall we make up our minds to read a few verses from our Bibles faithfully every day in Lent? Shall we make up our minds to say at least one prayer every day during Lent? If we prepare in faith, we shall most assuredly be blessed.

Prayer:

O God our Father, through the ages, and through the voices of your holy prophets, you have urged men to prepare for promised blessings. Help us so to keep this season of Lent as a time of preparation for Easter that we, too, may be blessed. Bless us with love for You, desire to walk in Christ's way, and opportunities to serve others for His sake. We ask our prayer in the Name of Him who prepared in Gethsemane, suffered on Calvary and lives for Eternity, Jesus Christ our Redeemer, Amen.

CHAPTER 48

Palm Sunday: the Triumphal Entry
God in Proclamation and Declaration

Scripture Reading: Luke 19:29-40

Key verse: Luke 19 verse 37: The whole multitude of the disciples began to rejoice and praise God with a loud voice.

Hymn: Ride on, ride on in majesty! (Henry Hart Milman 1791–1868).

When Jesus made His triumphal entry into Jerusalem the crowds were cheering enthusiastically and even throwing down their garments and palm branches in the road to honour Him as He passed.

The Triumphal Entry was a proclamation: Jesus was making a public declaration. The very act of entering Jerusalem in that way said something bold, challenging and inescapable about Jesus's Messiahship and His Kingdom. He was fulfilling the ancient prophecy of Zechariah (Zechariah 9:9): "Rejoice greatly, O daughter of Zion; shout, O daughter of Jerusalem: behold thy King cometh unto thee: he is just and having salvation; lowly and riding upon an ass, and upon a colt, the foal of an ass."

If Jesus had merely been the quiet, timid and cautious organiser of some small secret religious group, whose closely concealed ideas differed from those of the establishment – the people in power – the authorities would not have tried so hard to kill Him. If Jesus had not refuted their criticisms so brilliantly, and answered their trick questions so astutely – **in public** – they would not have hated Him so much. But Jesus Himself taught us that a light is meant to be put on a stand and seen, not concealed under a basket, that a city set on a hill cannot be hidden. The Gospel of Salvation which He brought is no timid, secret doctrine to be whispered about behind closed doors; it is for all the world. Christ's Gospel is like His Triumphal Entry on the first Palm Sunday – it is a declaration and a challenge. It is a universal proclamation of Christ the King and His Everlasting Kingdom.

One of the greatest problems in the world today is that evil flourishes when good men and women do nothing to stop it. If you saw a blind man walking near a cliff edge, you would either have to lead him away from the danger or else be morally responsible for his injuries when he fell. If good men and women do not protest at the sick and perverted rubbish that all too often passes for literature and entertainment today, they are morally responsible for the ill effects it has on society. If you see a thief breaking into your neighbour's house and do not report it to the Police, you are morally responsible for your neighbour's losses. If you know the glorious truth about the salvation which Jesus brings, and you do not tell people about it whenever you can, you are morally responsible for their ignorance.

We can also think of the Triumphal Entry on that first Palm Sunday as a symbol, or prototype, of Christ's triumphal entry into the believer's heart and mind, and, in fact, into every part of his, or her, life. Once a believer has accepted Christ, and the whole of that person's life has been changed infinitely for the better, then the Christ within us **has** to be proclaimed to the world.

As we think about the first Palm Sunday, let us resolve to proclaim what we as Christians believe in, just as our Lord proclaimed His Kingship. Let us declare our faith and our standards. The darker the world around us grows, and the lower its standards fall, so the higher must we lift the Christian banner, and the louder and more often must we proclaim Christ's truth to all men.

Prayer:

O Lord, our Heavenly Father, whose Great Son, Jesus Christ, declared His Eternal Kingship on the first Palm Sunday help us to declare for Him as willingly as He declared for us. Help us to proclaim our Christian faith and our Christian standards in the face of all danger and all opposition. Help us to welcome the Lord Jesus Christ into our hearts today, as His followers welcomed Him into Jerusalem long ago, for His Name's sake, Amen.

CHAPTER 49

The Meaning of Easter
God on the Cross

Scripture Reading: Luke 23:32-47

Key verse: Luke 23 verse 42: Jesus, Lord, remember me when Thou comest into Thy Kingdom.

Hymn: When I survey the wondrous Cross, (Isaac Watts, 1674–1748).

Countless Christian preachers and writers have contemplated their Lord's death on the Cross and have shared their thoughts with countless Christian congregations and Christian readers. Since that first great sermon which Peter preached after he was filled with the Power of the Holy Spirit after the Resurrection, the message of the Cross and its meaning has been proclaimed around the world. Yet every new sermon and every new book brings more light to shine on the inexhaustible and eternal truth.

Nearly 2,000 Easters have come and gone since Jesus died for us on Calvary, yet in all that time the good news of the Cross that saves sinners and destroys sin has never lost its breathtaking wonder or freshness.

What is the message? What is the meaning of the Cross? How can something that happened in Jerusalem 2,000 years ago change the lives of alcoholics, drug addicts, criminals and sinners today? **How?** A Just, Perfect and Righteous God cannot allow sin. Light cannot allow darkness in its presence. Heat cannot allow cold. Life cannot allow death. The very nature of the one **prevents** the other. Love cannot allow hatred, cruelty, greed or selfishness. They are simply and naturally incompatible. God loves mankind. God loves every unique individual human being with a love so tender, so strong and so compassionate, that He wants each one of us to live forever with Him in perfect fellowship and unimaginable joy.

When a human being chooses to sin, that man, or woman, automatically begins to separate himself, or herself, from the Love of God. Because God and sin are so totally incompatible, because sin **cannot** abide in the Presence of God, when we sin we suffer separation from the Divine Joy which God wills for us.

The Cross shows us the lengths to which God will go to bring us back again to Himself. There is no pain nor humiliation which

Divine Love will not bear in order to save us. That was the message which reached the dying thief who repented. Because sin is so terrible and destructive a thing God **cannot** condone it. He **cannot** say: "It doesn't matter." It does matter. It matters to Him because of the devastating and destructive effect it has on us, His beloved children. It matters so much to God that in the Person of Jesus, He even went to the Cross to put it right.

Prayer:

O loving and suffering Lord, we ask You to help us to understand the message of Your Cross, the meaning of Your suffering and the wonder of Your death for us. Help us to see the Cross as the cost and measure of sin, and help us to put sin far from us. Help us to see the Cross as the assurance of Your forgiveness and our new life, for the sake of Him who carried the Cross for us, Jesus Christ, our Lord, Amen.

CHAPTER 50

The Triumph of Easter
God in Resurrection and Life

Scripture Reading: Matthew 28:1-10

Key verse: Matthew 28 verse 10: Then said Jesus unto them, Be not afraid.

Hymn: Low in the grave He lay, (Robert Lowry 1826–1899).

The message and meaning of Easter is two-fold. There is the message of the Cross, which is suffering and death in order to bring about human redemption and salvation, and there is the message of the empty tomb which is victory and resurrection – abundant and eternal life.

When we realise that Christ died on the Cross for our sins that tells us of a Love beyond our power to conceive or to imagine. But when we realise that God raised Him up victorious on the First Easter Day that is Joy beyond joy and Wonder beyond wonders. **Jesus lives.** He is alive forever and ever. The greatest and most loving Friend any of us could ever dare to hope to have not only went to die for us – He lives for us.

In His Resurrection we not only have the divine assurance of our own immortality – Scripture has promised that because He lives we shall live also – but we have the indescribable joy of His unfailing presence.

Even in our ordinary earthly lives, the greatest happiness is to be found in good company. With loving families and faithful friends around us, all of life's pleasures are multiplied and increased. A solitary suspicious, lonely millionaire has far less happiness than the poorest member of a loving family which is struggling to buy its daily bread, or to meet its weekly bills. Looking at beautiful scenery in good company adds to the beauty. Watching an enjoyable film, or play, with friends increases our appreciation of the entertainment. Sharing a meal with those we love makes ordinary food into a feast. When the presence of loving human beings increases our enjoyment of ordinary, earthly things so much, think what the eternal company of Christ can do. Remember that Jesus loves us more than our nearest and dearest can love us, and He loves even the selfish more than the selfish can love themselves.

Joy and fear are opposites. Perfect love casts fear out. Love and joy are very close companions. If we let fear into our lives, it restricts and inhibits our joy. One of the greatest and most persistent of human fears is the fear of death. There are some sad and frightened people who seem to fear death so much that they never really enjoy life. Jesus, in our Key Verse, tells us not to be afraid. By His glorious Resurrection He has overcome death – for Himself and for us – and in His Victory we have the unfailing promise of eternal joy with Him.

Prayer:

O loving and glorious God, the Father of our Lord Jesus Christ, the Source of all life and the Conqueror of Death, we come before You at this Easter time to offer our humble thanks and praise. We praise and thank You, Father, for restoring our Lord Jesus Christ, Your Eternal Son, to everlasting life on that first Easter Day, and we ask that we may have such faith in Him that we, too, may share in His everlasting life and unending joy, for His Name's Sake, Amen.

CHAPTER 51

The Ascension
God the Son Returns to His Father

Scripture Reading: Luke 24:36-53

Key verse: Luke 24 verse 51: And it came to pass, while He blessed them, He was parted from them, and carried up into heaven.

Hymn: Where high the heavenly temple stands, (M. Bruce 1746-1767).

It is quite a popular thing with cynics, sceptics and opponents of Christianity to attack the Gospel at those points where Jesus entered and left our world. Like a besieging army around an impregnable city wall, or an impenetrable fortress, they think that the gates by which the Commander enters and leaves the citadel may provide weak spots in its defences.

Some people seem to find it hard to understand that Jesus was able to vanish from human sight and return to the glories of His Father's Kingdom. There are examples in the Old Testament of priests and prophets, outstanding men of God, who did not travel from time to eternity via the usual gates. Elijah the prophet was taken straight to God, and Enoch, one of the ancient patriarchs "walked with God, and he was not." There was also Melchizedek, the Priest-King of Salem, of whom Scripture records that he had "neither beginning of days nor end of life."

Those of you who are interested in reading what are sometimes called "Unsolved Mysteries" will already know about the strange disappearance of Benjamin Bathurst, of Captain Benjamin Spooner Briggs, his family and his crew from the **Mary Celeste.** You may know of the alleged **Philadelphia Experiment,** and you may have heard that perhaps there is something strange about the area known as **The Bermuda Triangle.** There may well be simple, straightforward, common-sense explanations for all of these alleged "mysteries" – yet vast numbers of people are ready to believe in them. Many who are all too ready to accept these accounts of unusual appearances or disappearances, are strangely reluctant to approach the Gospel account of the Lord's Ascension with the same open mindedness.

The most important event in the whole of human history was, is, and always will be the Incarnation of our Lord Jesus Christ. Nothing else would, or could, suffice to bring about the redemption of fallen humanity. God Himself, in the Person of Jesus broke into our world. He invaded this fallen, sin riddled earth of ours and saved it by that Divine Intervention. As the Scripture tells us : **God was in Christ reconciling the world to Himself.** There is **nothing** which the power of God the Omnipotent cannot accomplish. His Thoughts are not our thoughts, and His Ways are not our ways. The great Apostle Paul understood very well that there are Divine Mysteries that are beyond our present understanding. That God should choose to enter this world via the stable at Bethlehem and eventually leave it again by ascending until a cloud hid Him from the disciples' sight is part of the Divine Mystery.

The most eminent Professor of Physics in the world's most advanced University would be hard-pressed to give a complete and satisfactory explanation of the phenomenon which we call electric current, or electrical energy. A very young toddler is quite capable of understanding that when he presses the switch his bedroom light goes on. The greatest and wisest of our Christian philosophers, theologians and Bible scholars can never fully understand or explain the Divine Mysteries of the Incarnation and the Ascension, yet even a young child can know enough of Christ's Love to respond to it and accept it at his own level of understanding. If we choose to sit in the dark until we understand all the mysteries of electricity we shall sit in the dark forever!

Prayer:

Our loving heavenly Father, whose Son, Jesus Christ, came to earth to save us, help us at this Ascensiontide to think of all that He accomplished for us here before returning to You. Help us to accept that there will always be Divine Mysteries which our finite minds cannot fully understand during our earthly life. Grant us the wisdom to trust in You. Make us content to know that You will reveal to us in Your own perfect time everything that we need to understand in order to worship and serve You. For the sake of Him who returned to Your Glory at this time, Jesus Christ our Lord and our Redeemer, Amen.

CHAPTER 52

Whitsun
God the Holy Spirit

Scripture Reading : Acts 2:1-12

Key verse: Acts 2 verse 4: And they were all filled with the Holy Ghost.

Hymn: O Thou who camest from above, (Charles Wesley, 1707–1788).

After the Lord Jesus Christ had completed His earthly ministry and returned to His Father's Glory in Heaven, the Holy Spirit came to guide, inspire and strengthen the early disciples in their work of building the Church and spreading the Gospel. When the Church celebrates Whitsun, or Pentecost, we are celebrating the coming of the Holy Spirit to those first disciples.

Because, as human beings, our understanding is limited by our experiences of time and space, it is very hard for us to grasp the mystery of the Holy Trinity. We know about single, separate personalities – our own identity and the identities of others like us – and we can understand groups: families, friendship groups, classes, teaching sets and houses in school. What we find difficult to understand is how a Person can be both a Unity **and** a Trinity, as God is.

When Patrick of Ireland taught his listeners this truth, he showed them a shamrock with three leaves growing from a single stem. The three leaves were separate, but the stem united them into one plant. We can see something of this when we think of a really close and loving family. Each member is separate, but their love binds them together into an entity which has a kind of corporate life of its own: the Jones family, or the Smith family. Within this sacred mystery of the Trinity, the Holy Spirit is one vital element, along with God the Father and God the Son.

It is the Holy Spirit who leads us when we are willing to be led. When we pray for guidance, He is the best of all possible Guides. A ship can be navigated by the sun and stars, by a magnetic compass, by radar, and by radio beacons. In order to travel safely from port to port across wide seas and oceans, the ship depends upon something greater than itself. The compass responds to the magnetic field of the earth. The stars, which appear so tiny when viewed from the earth, are vast masses of blazing gas, light years distant. The navigational radio beacon may well be transmitting from hundreds of miles away. The Pole Star, on which much navigation depends, is not only greater than any ship – it is far greater than the whole earth! We cannot even begin to compare the unlimited power and wisdom of the Holy Spirit with that of an individual human being. The differences are too great. Yet we can be certain of this: the Holy Spirit will guide all of us who are willing to be guided far more surely and far more faithfully than the Pole Star guides a ship. It is our willingness to be guided which is the sole criterion. Despite His unlimited power and His loving desire to guide and help us, the Holy Spirit will not force or coerce us in any way. God, who has all power, asks and invites human beings, who have practically no power at all. He pleads with us to come to Him. The power of His pleading and the infinite depth of His Divine Love are revealed on Calvary.

Once we have realised that, and accepted the Divine Invitation to salvation in Christ, we are ready to seek the Holy Spirit's guidance for the rest of our lives – not only on earth, but throughout eternity.

Prayer:

O most holy and blessed Trinity, God the Father, Son and Holy Spirit, we come before You asking forgiveness, renewal of life, and guidance. We pray that the Holy Spirit may enter our lives, cleanse them from all that is unworthy and lead us in the way You would have us go. Help us to trust You in our voyage through life, as a wise sailor trusts his compass and the Pole Star. Lead us into the way of truth, light and goodness, for Jesus' sake, Amen.

INDEX OF HYMNS

INDEX OF BIBLE READINGS